D0188813

FORTRESS
INTRODUCTION TO
LUTHERANISM

Also from Fortress Press

CARL E. BRAATEN
Principles of Lutheran Theology

CARL E. BRAATEN AND ROBERT W. JENSON, EDITORS
Christian Dogmatics, 2 volumes

ERIC W. GRITSCH AND ROBERT W. JENSON
*Lutheranism: The Theological Movement and
Its Confessional Writings*

DAVID A. GUSTAFSON
*Lutherans in Crisis:
The Question of Identity in the American Republic*

TIMOTHY F. LULL, EDITOR
Martin Luther's Basic Theological Writings

WILLIAM R. RUSSELL
*Luther's Theological Testament:
The Schmalkald Articles*
(forthcoming)

FORTRESS
INTRODUCTION TO
LUTHERANISM

Eric W. Gritsch

Fortress Press ◇ Minneapolis

BX
8018
.G75
1994

To Emilia

FORTRESS INTRODUCTION TO LUTHERANISM

Copyright © 1994 Augsburg Fortress. All rights reserved. Except for brief quotations in critical articles or reviews, no part of this book may be reproduced in any manner without prior written permission from the publisher. Write to: Permissions, Augsburg Fortress, 426 S. Fifth St., Box 1209, Minneapolis, MN 55440.

Scripture quotations, unless otherwise noted, are from the New Revised Standard Version Bible, copyright © 1989 by the Division of Christian Education of the National Council of Churches in the USA and used by permission.

Other credits may be found on p. 158.

Cover design: Patricia Boman
Interior design: The Book Company/Wendy Calmenson

Library of Congress Cataloging-in-Publication Data
Gritsch, Eric W.
    Fortress introduction to Lutheranism/Eric W. Gritsch.
        p.   cm.
    Includes bibliographical references and index.
    ISBN 0-8006-2780-6 (alk. paper)   :
    1. Lutheran Church—History. 2. Lutheran Church—Doctrines.
I. Title.
BX8018.G75   1994   93-21891
284.1—dc20   CIP

The paper used in this publication meets the minimum requirements of American National Standard for Information Sciences—Permanence of Paper for Printed Library Materials, ANSI Z329.48-1984. ∞™

Manufactured in the U.S.A.   AF 1-2780

98   97   96   95   94   1   2   3   4   5   6   7   8   9   10

C O N T E N T S

CONCORDIA COLLEGE LIBRARY
2811 NE HOLMAN ST.
PORTLAND, OR 97211-6099

Part Two: Challenge

LIST OF ILLUSTRATIONS

PREFACE

What does it mean to be "Lutheran"? Some Lutherans still consider themselves members of the sixteenth-century movement led by Luther to reform the Roman Catholic Church; they also work for the reform of the church catholic, hoping for an ever greater measure of Christian unity. Other Lutherans have accepted the institutionalization of the movement and have joined the various Lutheran churches around the world, totalling nearly sixty million members. Most Lutherans, however, are confused about their historical roots, doctrinal affirmations, and ethical directives.

This book offers a distillation of Lutheran history (Part One) and Lutheran teachings (Part Two) to help readers give meaning to the designation "Lutheran." The historical Lutheran legacy is presented with an eye on what happened to the original Lutheran affirmations summarized in *The Book of Concord.* Then this legacy is set forth as a challenge addressed to contemporary Lutherans with an ear open to what my contemporaries are thinking and saying in the places where they make their living. Appendix A offers a sketch of the origins and content of Lutheran normative teachings, known as the "Lutheran Confessions" collected in *The Book of Concord.*

Much of this book has been presented in classes, seminars, and at various teaching events in Lutheran and other churches. I have condensed my experience and learning for those who, like me, have been enriched in their Christian faith by being Lutheran.

A manuscript page of Luther's translation

LEGACY

Luther as the "German Hercules"

The Luther Event

---◇---

Breakthrough and Breakaway

The time of Martin Luther (November 10, 1483 to February 18, 1546) was one of restlessness, and Martin Luther embodied the spirit of his time. Christianity had been divided in 1054 into a Western church led by the pope in Rome and an Eastern church led by the patriarch of Constantinople. A rebirth (renaissance) of pre-Christian art and a concentration on earthly life (humanism) challenged old traditions in the West. European exploration of the lands across the oceans opened up new ways of thinking, trading, and comparing life-styles. The rise of Islam in southern Europe threatened established Christendom, despite the many terrorizing crusades led by Christians against the followers of Mohammed. The invention of an efficient printing press by Johann Gutenberg in Mainz in the 1450s had radically changed old ways of communicating. The Fugger bank in Augsburg had put Germany on the map of economic superpowers; the printing press created the world of paper money.

Papal power in Rome had been severely curtailed by schism between 1309 and 1415. For more than a century, one pope in Rome and one in Avignon, France, competed for jurisdiction. Papal power, though bruised and weakened, returned to Rome when the council of bishops and reform movements like those of John Wycliffe in Oxford and Jan Hus in Prague gained influence in the church. Once more established in Rome under a single pope, the papacy now demanded greater obedience from both clergy and laity; the distance between church leaders and the people widened. The laity sank into a mire of superstition, often fueled by fear of punishment after death. The sacrament of penance became the principal tool by which the hierarchy ruled. Confessors in oral confession kept penitents in line by citing the church as the only means of escaping eternal punishment for earthly sins. As a result, life was based on the "if–then" condition: if I do such and such for God— that is, for the church—then I will endure less punishment, both now and after death, for sins I commit. The church first tolerated, then gradually encouraged, the popular belief in purgatory. Purgatory was located somewhere between heaven and earth; it purified, by means of fire, all sinners on their way to eternal life.

Born and raised in Saxony, near the Czech border, Luther was encouraged by his parents to become a lawyer, for lawyers earned a fortune from the noble rich and quickly rose to the top of society. If that didn't work, his father Hans reasoned that Martin could marry a rich woman. Young Luther, surrounded by caring relatives and friends, received a solid education in both academics and traditional religion. He enrolled in the law school in Erfurt. But, while on a walk in the Saxon countryside, the twenty-one-year-old law student was frightened by a thunderstorm and cried out, "Help, St. Anna (grandmother of Jesus), and I will become a monk!" She did, and he did. Two weeks later he joined the order of the Augustinian Hermits.

As a monk Luther underwent a gruelling schedule of academic work and prayer. Both friends and enemies agreed that Martin was one of the best monks. But he was constantly plagued by inner turmoil (called *Anfechtung* in German). Having grown up under the "if–then" condition of Christian living in its many variations, he shared some of the superstitions of the people and feared punishment in this or the next life for commiting sins. Could he ever do enough to earn God's love? Would God really save him from sin? Indeed, did a gracious God exist, since one only heard about a wrathful one in church? Luther consistently flunked private confession; whenever he was absolved from a confessed sin he thought of a new one to confess.

Like many Lutheran seminarians today, Luther went through an identity crisis while training for the priesthood. Private confession at the time was like clinical pastoral education today: the supervisor/father confessor demanded from the candidate even greater efforts to please God—fasting, praying, working harder, etc.—in an effort to make sure of the candidate's identity. Because Luther had given all that was in him to give, urging him to try harder only deepened his despair. He ended up being frightened at the sound of a falling leaf (Lev. 26:36). The general of the Augustinian order, Johann von Staupitz, finally gave him a direct order: "You will become a doctor of Holy Scripture." Luther had no choice but to obey; if he gave up, he would lose himself in despair. Staupitz' psychological experiment worked: Luther was told to rely on a new vocation just when he was on the verge of losing his identity. He was to become a theologian of the Bible and so could return to the very source of Christianity: God's revelation in Christ attested to in Holy Scripture. The daily grind of study, worship, and teaching saved Luther's life.

When Luther dug deeper into Holy Scripture, he rediscovered what had long been ignored: one is reconciled with God by having faith rather than by any moral effort. "The one who is righteous will live by faith" (Rom. 1:17 referencing Hab. 2:4), and the object of that faith is Jesus Christ. Luther realized that the apostle Paul focused all his teaching on Christ crucified and resurrected. For Paul, the advent of Christ was "the fullness of time" when together Jews and Gentiles could call God their loving Father who put his Holy Spirit into faithful hearts and liberated them from the slavery of sin (Gal. 4:4-6). When Christ is the center of one's life, Luther told his students, one has the correct theology, because it points to Christ as the power that comes from outside. No inner disposition or external good work has that power—it comes from Jesus alone.

This concept was foreign to the teaching and practice prevalent in the church of Luther's time. Both academic theologians and common clergy had compromised what Luther called the biblical center by claiming that salvation from sin is a process of cooperation between divine grace and human efforts. "Do good during the week," parishioners were told, "and then come to church to add sacramental grace to your efforts to please God. Your credit, based on your natural ability to do good, will join with God's gift to make you a true child of God."

Some bishops in Germany abused this pastoral advice by urging people to trust the church to help their efforts to please God, and started to sell indulgences. Ever since the Crusades which sought to liberate the holy land from Islam, the church had awarded indulgences granting forgiveness of many sins to those who fought there. At that time paper money and printed indulgences made the increase in the traffic of indulgences possible. Permits were sold that granted forgiveness for sins not yet committed, such as eating meat on Friday. Other indulgences even promised, for the payment of large sums, to release deceased relatives from purgatory. Johann Tetzel, a Dominican priest and successful indulgences salesman, appeared at the Saxon border to sell indulgences with the slogan, "As soon as the coin in the coffer rings, the soul out of purgatory springs."

Luther became famous on October 31, 1517, when he posted his Ninety-Five Theses on the door of the Wittenberg Castle Church to call for a debate on the indulgences abuses. Since Rome had collected a lot of money for the construction of a cathedral for St. Peter through the sale of indulgences in Germany, many Germans allied themselves with Luther in his critique. Moreover, many indulgences had been sold on behalf of a bishop who made a large payment to Rome and consequently was installed as archbishop.

Rome refused to heed an obscure monk from Germany who happened to be a biblical theologian at the newly founded university in Wittenberg, an insignificant academic institution. Instead, Rome requested that the Elector Frederick of Saxony, Luther's territorial ruler, hand over the professor to Roman authorities for punishment. Elector Frederick refused politely and insisted that Rome must not silence Luther without proper debate.

Movement and Institution

Elector Frederick was one of seven German princes empowered to elect the Holy Roman Emperor—a title used since A.D. 800 to symbolize unity between church and state—and he therefore had considerable influence in the government of the empire, especially since he had cast

Johann Tetzel

the decisive vote in favor of electing the Spanish candidate, Charles V, in 1519. As a result, the new Holy Roman Emperor owed Frederick favors, which is why Luther was permitted hearings in Germany rather than Rome.

In 1518, he had a hearing in Augsburg before the Roman cardinal Cajetan, who refused to debate him; in 1519, Luther debated the Dominican theologian Johann Eck in Leipzig. The Leipzig debate disclosed how far Luther had moved away from the teachings of his church. At issue was the thirteenth thesis: Is the papacy a divine institution (Eck's position), or is it the result of human development (Luther's contention)? Eck persuaded Luther to admit that he agreed with Jan Hus of Prague, a reformer who had been burned at the stake in 1415 for the heresy of denying that the papacy was divinely instituted. The umpire then declared Eck the winner of the debate.

Most Germans, however, ignored the umpire's decision. Luther was their hero who had stood up against a money-hungry Roman papacy. People from all strata of society—peasants, intellectuals, merchants, and a number of nobles hoping to gain more power—now joined his reform movement. Even priests and monks began to realize that Luther was not an innovator but rather a defender of the ancient Christian teachings that focused on Christ. He wrote several treatises to undergird this growing reform movement. What struck his readers as most important was his assertion, made in 1520, that before God all who have been baptized are equal and therefore all are potentially priest, bishop or pope. Only one Christian estate exists, according to Luther. All Christians are commissioned by their baptism into a ministry on earth until Christ's second coming; this ministry is carried out either through a full-time, lifelong priesthood or through other vocations. To be an ordained priest means merely to preside at the assembly of the baptized and to support them in their various ministries to the world.

Rome's response to Luther and his cause was totally hostile. Luther was accused of heresy, an accusation endorsed particularly by the German Dominican order, which defended the church's official teachings and disliked the Augustinian Hermits in Erfurt. A papal commission in Rome studied Luther's writings and concluded that he had transgressed official doctrine and was required to recant. Luther received the official notice which ordered him to recant within sixty days of its receipt. On December 10, 1520, he participated in a protest demonstration held by faculty and students of Wittenberg University, and threw the papal documents, as well as some other Roman writings, into the bonfire.

Luther's earlier appeal to be heard by a General Council—the traditional forum attended by bishops—had been unsuccessful. Rome wanted him to recant or be condemned a heretic. Luther refused to recant. On January 3, 1521, he was excommunicated by papal bull (a document so named because the pope sealed it with his insignia), which called him "a boar in the vineyard of the Lord," trampling down what God had given the church on earth. The bull ordered all of Luther's followers to recant, and all his books to be burned; all Luther's functions as priest and professor were ordered revoked.

Elector Frederick (later called "the Wise") was not convinced that his favorite professor had had a fair hearing, so he did not implement the bull's orders. Luther continued to function as both priest and professor in Wittenberg. Frederick persuaded Emperor Charles V to hear Luther at the Diet of Worms, the next assembly of German princes that would be held in April 1521. Papal diplomats tried in vain to change the emperor's mind. One felt completely frustrated, and, in a secret message to Rome, reported that nine-tenths of the Germans praised Luther while the other tenth cried "Death to the Roman Curia!" People tore down and often burned the papal bull of excommunication wherever it had been posted.

Luther appeared before the Diet on April 17, and was asked again to recant. He requested, and was granted, one day to prepare his answer. The next day he declared he could not and would not recant unless persuaded by Scripture and reason. His conscience, he stated, was captive to the word of God rather than to popes or councils. "I cannot do otherwise," he said. "Here I stand. May God help me. Amen." This declaration canceled further sessions of the Diet for several days because most delegates were angry and confused. Some delegates, though, were impressed by Luther. Vain attempts to change Luther's mind were made in private negotiations. Elector Frederick, who had already taken measures to assure Luther's safety, recommended he leave Worms. On his way back to Wittenberg, Luther was "kidnapped" by some of Frederick's men and conveyed to the Wartburg, one of Frederick's castles in the Thuringian forest.

A month after Luther left, on May 26, 1521, the Diet of Worms issued an "edict" of condemnation against Luther, charging him and his followers with high treason. Every citizen was ordered to capture the "demon in monk's garb" or face trial for the same crimes.

Safely hidden at the Wartburg, Luther was known as "Knight George" to conceal his identity. He grew a beard, dressed as a knight, avoided conversations with strangers, and continued to write. He began to translate the Bible, starting with the New Testament, which appeared in 1522 as the "September Bible." He also stayed in contact with a few special friends in Wittenberg, especially his closest friend Philipp Melanchthon, a young humanist and linguist.

There was growing confusion in Wittenberg during the time of Luther's exile at the Wartburg. Radicals like Andreas Karlstadt, dean of the university and a sudden convert, tried to push Luther's cause. An influx of street preachers proclaimed the imminent end of the world. Some called themselves prophets and reported seeing visions influenced by the Holy Spirit. On Christmas Day, 1521, Karlstadt tried to integrate all these dissident views by presiding at an "evangelical Mass"—a simple service focusing on the words of the Eucharist—without using traditional vestments. The common cup was offered to everyone. (Offering the common cup had been prohibited since 1215; only priests could handle the holy elements, so as to safeguard them from abuse.) Although almost all the twenty-five hundred Wittenbergers attended the service, many felt that Karlstadt and his followers were going too far too fast. Melanchthon, worried and cautious, informed Luther of the events.

Luther became very concerned about what was happening in Wittenberg. He labeled the radicals "swarmers" *(Schwärmer)* who, like wild bees, sting without reason and should be driven off. On March 6, 1522, he disobeyed Frederick's request to stay at the Wartburg and returned to Wittenberg, declaring that his pastoral duties were more important than his personal safety. By preaching a series of Lenten sermons emphasizing the necessity of law and order while not neglecting reform, Luther succeeded in restoring peace and order. The radicals disappeared, and Karlstadt married and moved to another town.

Martin Luther, a condemned heretic at age forty-two, married a twenty-six-year-old apostate nun, Katherine von Bora, on June 13, 1525. Prince Johann—brother and successor to Frederick, who had died in May—gave the newlyweds the Augustinian cloister in which Luther had lived for so many years and which by now the other monks had left. The Luther household, eventually filled with ten children (six of their own, four adopted on the death of relatives) and numerous house guests, became a model parsonage and a center of Wittenberg life.

Luther gradually transformed Wittenberg into a Lutheran stronghold and model for other communities in Germany. By 1523 the medieval Mass had turned into an "evangelical Mass" that kept much of the old, but focused on the use of the German language, preaching, Holy Communion, and congregational participation through singing. Liturgical reforms were accompanied by new catechetical programs. Visitations to the surrounding countryside, sponsored by Elector Frederick, had revealed dismal conditions: most priests were uneducated, lay people were often illiterate, and a common, creative Christian lifestyle was almost nonexistent. As a result, Luther, who was convinced that the laity shared the responsibility of ministry with the clergy, drafted two catechisms in 1529: a Large Catechism for teachers, and a Small Catechism for children.

Charles V was not able to enforce the edict passed by the Diet of Worms. He needed the support of the German princes, including Lutheran princes, to defend the empire against the attacking Turks, who were finally repulsed in Vienna in 1529. He and the pope agreed to settle the issue of Lutheranism at a religious council to be called by the pope.

Meanwhile Lutheranism was spreading rapidly. In order to do *something* to achieve Christian unity, the emperor convened another diet at Augsburg in 1530 to hear the divergent views and opinions. Seven Lutheran territorial princes and two cities submitted a "Confession of Faith" (later known as the "Augsburg Confession") on June 25, 1530. The Augsburg Confession was a collaborative work drafted by Luther's friend and colleague Philipp Melanchthon and the consultation of others. It affirms basic articles of faith and doctrine, such as the dogma of the Trinity as a central universal Christian affirmation and "justification by faith alone" as the biblical center of Lutheranism. The Confession advocates Christian unity and invites discussion of abuses of power by the church. Lutherans wanted to clarify, as the conclusion of the Confession asserts, that they "have introduced nothing, either in doctrine or in ceremonies, that is contrary to Holy Scripture or the universal Christian Church."

Immediately after reading the Augsburg Confession, Emperor Charles V appointed a group of theologians headed by a papal representative to assess the document. They reported their conclusions in the "Confutation," read to the diet on August 3, 1530. Although they accepted some of the twenty-eight articles of the Augsburg Confession, such as those on the Trinity and on secular government (the latter "with pleasure" because it affirmed law and order), they rejected the basic

The Castle Church at Wittenberg

The Wartburg (castle)

Pope Leo X

Title page of the papal bull
issued against Luther

Elector Frederick the Wise

1526
VIVENTIS·POTVIT·DVRERIVS·ORA·PHILIPPI
MENTEM·NON·POTVIT·PINGERE·DOCTA
MANVS

Emperor Charles V

Philipp Melanchthon

Andreas Bodenstein (Karlstadt)

Title page from Luther's Small Catechism

Katherine von Bora

Public reading of the Augsburg Confession

Lutheran position represented by the articles that dealt with justification and with rejection of divinely instituted church structures. Melanchthon responded with a long "Apology" (meaning "defense"), trying to be as conciliatory as possible.

Melanchthon and his disciples, known as "Philippists," continued to dialogue with some Roman theologians, including one cardinal. But neither Rome nor Luther accepted any compromises—especially on the important issue of whether the papacy alone should exercise teaching authority. It became clear that the Lutheran reform movement could survive only outside the Roman institution.

In 1520, when Catholic bishops refused to join the Lutheran reform movement, Luther called upon Lutheran territorial princes to become "emergency bishops" *(Notbischöfe)*. Since being baptized is as good as being a bishop, he contended, why not have experienced baptized politicians take over the reins of the church until the church produced its own good bishops? What resulted was the formation of a territorial church.

The institutionalization of Lutheran reform in Scandinavia began in 1536, when King Christian III of Denmark declared the Augsburg Confession the basis of a new Lutheran church supplanting Roman authority. Catholic bishops were dismissed and Lutheran bishops were installed. Norway, then a part of Denmark, followed suit, as did Sweden and Finland in 1593, after some struggle.

◇ ———————————————————————————— ◇

A Man for Few Seasons

Luther's cause was espoused after 1522 by other reformers who advocated more radical change. Thomas Müntzer, a pastor in Saxony and one of Luther's disciples, promoted the violent overthrow of the ruling princes because they opposed the God-willed egalitarian society he envisioned. He joined rebelling peasants and was executed in 1525 in an event advocated and blessed by Luther.

Ulrich Zwingli began a reformation in 1522 in Zurich, Switzerland, with the help of city magistrates. He removed all traces of Roman Catholicism, including all ornamentation in the churches, all music, and all liturgical rituals. He declared a "crusade" against the opposing Swiss Catholics, and died in battle against them in 1531 in Kappel.

One Zwinglian group formed a fellowship of Christians noted for its rejection of infant baptism in favor of "believers' baptism" of committed adults and by its insistence of total separation of church and state. They were nicknamed "Anabaptists" (from the Greek, meaning "rebaptizers"). Under the leadership of the Dutch reformer Menno Simons, they would become known as Mennonites. Another and more fanatic group of Dutch Anabaptists occupied the German city of Münster in 1535 and transformed it into their idea of a biblical city, marked by polygamy, economic communism, and other so-called scriptural characteristics. They were defeated by a combined armed force of Catholics and Lutherans and were executed that same year.

Luther, who spent his final years deepening his understanding of Scripture and battling the forces of both the right (Rome) and the left (the *Schwärmer*), saw in the person of Müntzer and the fanatics of Münster the embodiments of Satan which should be overcome by force.

TOMAS MVNCER PREDIGER ZV ALSTET IN DVRINGEN

Thomas Müntzer

What upset him most was the Zwinglian rejection of the traditional interpretation of Holy Communion, according to which Christ is bodily present, even though that presence cannot be explained. Zwingli, and later John Calvin in Geneva, insisted on some explanation of Holy Communion. Zwingli contended that the Eucharist is only a memorial of Christ's death, and Calvin asserted that Christ is only spiritually present in some non-corporeal fashion and should be celebrated only on a few specific days during the year. When even Karlstadt, Luther's colleague and dean of the university, advocated a similar position, Luther decided all this was *Schwärmerei* inspired by Satan rather than the Holy Spirit.

Quite tolerant of Jews at first, Luther became infuriated when he heard in 1539 that they were trying to convert Christians. He became convinced that they too had become part of Satan's fifth column, undermining Christianity's final reformation before Christ's second coming. Here Luther succumbed to a malicious anti-Semitism that had plagued the church for centuries. He argued in emotional treatises that God had abandoned the Jews and that, therefore, Christians should not only shun them but drive them from the land. He went so far as to recommend specific steps that the political authorities could take against the Jews, such as establishing labor camps and destroying the synagogues. He saw Jews, papists, Turks, Zwinglians, and all other *Schwärmer* as the final *Anfechtung*, the final violent sign presaging the end of the world.

He often used earthy language to vent his frustration at these final tribulations: "I am like a ripe stool, and the world is like a gigantic anus, and we are about to let go of each other" he said at one of his final table talks. But this language discloses a humor—indeed, the humor of the gallows—that was deeply imbedded in his child-like faith in the God who was in charge of the world no matter how bad things were. His sense of humor grew out of his biblical studies, especially of his favorite books: Genesis, Psalms, the Gospel of John, and the Pauline letters. The Jewish patriarchs taught him how faith liberates one from the world's many cares, the Psalms showed him how a suffering people survives wrestling with God, the Gospel of John revealed how Jesus could make fun of his enemies, and Paul showed him how to minister, as a fool for Christ, in the midst of adversity. Luther saw himself as a part of this peculiar history of salvation, and labeled himself a court jester in the guise of a monk who spoke the truth regarding the meaning of all human existence in the shadow of the crucified Jesus of Nazareth. Except for his apocalyptic views, Luther retained a joyful attitude toward life. Music, babies, his dog Klutz, his wife Katherine, nature, and above all, the word of God, kept Luther sane.

Lutheranism did not fare well during the final years of Luther's life. In the 1530s, Catholics formed a military league to fight against Lutheran princes; the Lutherans responded by forming the Schmalkald League, named after the city in which they met in 1537. The assembled Lutheran princes asked Luther to draft a statement showing what they should fight or indeed die for.

Luther, very ill at the time of the formation of the Schmalkald League, composed a theological last will and testament later known as the "Schmalkald Articles." He reaffirmed his belief in the trinitarian creed and total trust in what God had done in Christ rather than what believers can do to earn their salvation. Citing Paul, he confessed that Jesus "was handed over to death for our trespasses and was raised for our justification" (Rom. 4:25).

According to Luther, this is "the first and chief article of faith. Nothing in this article can be given up or compromised, even if heaven and earth and things temporal should be destroyed." Because Rome had rejected this very center of the gospel, Luther declared, "The pope is the real Antichrist," and that an ecumenical council should be convened to condemn Rome. He once again listed the issues he felt should be discussed by "learned and sensible minds" for the sake of a healthy church: sin, law, penitence, the gospel, sacraments, ministry, and the church.

Forty-three theologians, pastors, and "superintendents" (the Latin root means "bishop") signed the Schmalkald Articles. Melanchthon appended a conciliatory note to his signature, in which he endorsed the notion of a papacy provided it was viewed as a human rather than a divine institution. He made this concession "for the sake of peace and general unity among the Christians who are now under him [the pope] and who may be in the future" (*The Book of Concord* 316–17). Later in 1537, in a treatise on the power and primacy of the pope, he explained his position further: if Rome kept insisting on its divine right, it belonged to the kingdom of the Antichrist, and Christians ought then to leave Rome's jurisdiction (*BC* 327:41).

Gall and kidney stones, angina pectoris, insomnia, migraines, and old age finally overcame Luther in the early morning hours of February 18, 1546, in his native city of Eisleben. There he attempted to reconcile two feuding noble families. His final written words concerned the difficulty of fathoming the true meaning of texts, biblical texts in particular: "We are all beggars, that is true."

Luther was a formidable figure. His life and work made a difference in world history. His literary legacy is staggering: he produced more

Death of Martin Luther (sketch)

than 450 treatises, some quite voluminous; more than three thousand sermons and twenty-six hundred letters; and nearly seven thousand "table talks." The Weimar edition of Luther's works, already consisting of over one hundred oversized volumes, is still incomplete, for not everything has yet been traced. An international Congress for Luther Research, meeting periodically, assures continued interest in Martin Luther and continues to contribute pieces to a growing "Lutherania." Luther was truly a man for few seasons.

The Elector Johann Frederick of Saxony surrounded by the Wittenberg Reformers

The Aborted Reformation

---◇---

Away from Rome

When the pope and the emperor agreed in 1546 to settle the religious controversy by the use of force, Lutheranism was on its way to becoming a church independent of Rome. Luther, and especially Philipp Melanchthon, had never advocated such a move, but history took over. The emperor declared war on Lutheran territories, and the pope called a General Council (the formal teaching authority of the church) to convene in 1545 in Trent, Italy, to condemn Lutheranism.

The Protestant Schmalkald League was defeated by imperial troops in 1547, and forced to accept a peace treaty favoring Catholic territories. The Peace of Augsburg, signed in 1555, used Luther's suggestion of 1520 to forge a formula declaring, "He who rules a region is in charge of its religion" *(cuius regio, eius religio)*, thus establishing territorial churches under the leadership of the territory's rulers. Luther's emergency measures were transformed into a controversial political reality. By 1555, German territories were split into two official religious communities: Roman Catholic and the churches of the Augsburg Confession.

Once Lutheran princes in Germany were given the right to establish Lutheranism as the religion of their land, the state, or "people's church,"

(Volkskirche), was born which, since politicians do not easily yield power once they have it, would remain in force until the end of World War I. The princes had become the heads of the church, "supreme bishops" *(summi episcopoi)* as the law stated it. As such, they were of course concerned with unity in their territories. The drive for unity, however, usually turned into a drive for uniformity undergirded by law and enforced by the state.

Simultaneous with the formation of Lutheran confessional churches in Germany, Scandinavia, and some East European territories (Poland, Hungary, and Czechoslovakia had Lutheran minorities protected by the ruling princes), came the formal refutation of Lutheranism by the Roman Catholic Council of Trent (1545–1563, with interruptions). Many of the Council's decisions were drafted by the newest religious order, the "Society of Jesus"—called "Jesuits"—founded by Ignatius of Loyola, a radical priest. (Pope Paul had quickly approved the order, since, besides the three traditional vows of chastity, poverty, and obedience to the head of the order, the Society imposed a fourth vow: unconditional obedience to the papacy.) Jesuits were well-trained theologians whom the bishops employed as advisors at the Council.

The first sessions of the Council quickly established that Rome considered the Bible and the Roman tradition to be the ultimate teaching authority. By adding "tradition" as a source of revelation (though not above the word of God in Scripture), the Council opened the way for what would later be called "theological extensions" of Scripture, such as the immaculate conception of Mary. (There is no explicit biblical evidence for this doctrine, but it was adduced, or "extended," from the notion of Mary's virginity.)

The other sessions of the Council rejected the Lutheran insistence on "justification" as the center of the Gospel, calling it just one step in the process of salvation which is aided by human efforts and administered by the church's sacramental grace. Although it never mentioned Luther or any other reformer by name, the Council made it clear that no Lutheran proposals for reform were welcome. But it did condemn many abuses like the indulgences traffic Luther had attacked and the immoral conduct of bishops and clergy.

The Council's decisions were printed in a Trentine Catechism so that Jesuits, parish priests, or any other group in the church, could begin to bring Lutherans and other schismatics back to Rome—what historians have called the "Counter-Reformation." Catholic princes quickly enforced these decisions. Rome created an "Index of Prohibited Books," to try to eradicate Luther's writings and thus enforce what the Edict of Worms had tried in 1521. The prohibition was only partially successful, however, since printers were by now numerous and more concerned with profits than with commands from Rome.

The Lutheran reform movement—grounded in academic freedom, encouraged by the Saxon princes, and convinced that, as Luther put it, the church was "always to be reformed" *(ecclesia semper reformanda)*—enjoyed healthy theological debates and was shaped in part by various controversies. In the 1530s, Johann Agricola, one of Luther's students, declared that faith needed no laws, since believers would naturally do what needed to be done for the neighbor. This was a kind of antinomianism (from the Greek *nomos*, meaning "law") that was an enduring problem in Christianity.

Another group of Luther's disciples, led by Matthias Flacius, claimed to be "authentically Lutheran" because of its abolition of everything Catholic. Known as "Gnesiolutherans" (from the Greek *gnesio*, meaning "authentic"), they rejected all things not essential for salvation, such as liturgy, making the sign of the cross, etc. as "adiaphora" (meaning "things neither commanded nor prohibited by God"). This controversy lasted from the late 1540s to the early 1550s. The Gnesiolutherans were the most anti-Roman Catholic Lutherans, and were closely allied with those Lutherans who were unwilling to compromise with other Protestants, especially Calvinists, on the issue of Christ's real presence in the Eucharist. The Gnesiolutheran pastor Johann Timann labeled all compromisers on the Eucharist "crypto-Calvinists."

Some Lutheran theologians, like Georg Major, argued that good works are necessary for salvation; others, like Nicholas von Amsdorf, took the opposite view. This so called Majorist controversy raged in the 1550s.

During the 1550s and 1560s, a Gnesiolutheran group from Wittenberg University fought theologians from the nearby University of Jena over another enduring problem in Christianity; whether or not human will is free to cooperate with God's grace in attaining salvation. This so-called synergist debate (from Greek *synergoi*, meaning "with works")

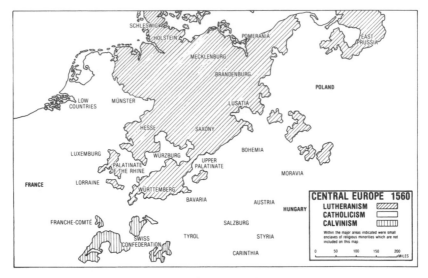

Central Europe, 1560

was related to another controversy involving Andreas Osiander, a professor at the Prussian University of Königsberg. Osiander claimed that
justification by faith occurs through a mystical in-dwelling of Christ in
the human heart, thus bypassing the external word. The government
countered this Osiandrian assertion by enforcing the Lutheran doctrine
that Christ is mediated by the external word audible in preaching and
visible in sacraments. Chaplain Johann Funck, of the Prussian court,
was executed for insisting that one can be saved without the external
word of God.

   There were, then, two main feuding parties in Lutheranism by the
late sixteenth century: the Gnesiolutherans, who were convinced they
were preserving the teaching of Luther; and the Philippists, the more
conciliatory faction led by Philipp Melanchthon until his death in 1560.
Melanchthon had been upset over the fierce quarrels among Lutherans,
and vainly tried to reconcile the feuding factions by rewriting the 1530
Augsburg Confession in 1540. This "altered" Augsburg Confession was
rejected by the Lutheran territories.

   A middle party, led by Swabian theologians at the University of
Tübingen and the renowned bishop and theologian from Brunswick,

Martin Chemnitz, then tried to mediate by drafting a "Formula of Concord." In 1573, Jakob Andreä, the chancellor of Tübingen, preached six sermons based on a Formula of Concord. Prince August of Saxony joined the effort by simply dismissing most of the teaching theologians warring in his territory.

Finally, in 1577, the Formula of Concord was accepted and adopted. It was added to the other already accepted Lutheran Confessions and was printed together in *The Book of Concord*, which contained the Apostles' Creed, the Nicene Creed, and the Athanasian Creed; Luther's two Catechisms (1529); the Augsburg Confession (1530); Melanchthon's "Apology," (his defense of the Augsburg Confession); Luther's Schmalkald Articles (1537); Melanchthon's treatise on the pope (1539); and the Formula of Concord (1577).

The Book of Concord, published in 1580 on the fiftieth anniversary of the Augsburg Confession and acknowledged as the Lutheran confessional norm by fifty-one ruling nobles, thirty-eight cities, and about eight thousand theologians, was intended as a testimony to the work of Luther who had brought his beloved homeland into the "unadulterated light of God's holy Gospel . . . out of papistic superstition and darkness," as the preface puts it. It was meant to be ecumenical, in the sense that, as the preface states, it did "not manufacture anything new" but rather abided in the faith of the universal Christian church. (*BC* 3:13). The preface also expressed the hope that Lutherans would henceforth be spared Rome's and other adversaries' accusation of being uncertain in their faith, for their faith was based "on the prophetic and apostolic Scriptures and is comprehended in the three Creeds as well as in the Augsburg Confession" (*BC* 13).

The subscribers to *The Book of Concord* declared that they were "minded by the grace of the Holy Spirit to abide and remain unanimously in this confession of faith and to regulate all religious controversies and their explanations according to it" (*BC* 14). Moreover, they called for a proper distinction between "needless and unprofitable contentions and necessary controversy." Necessary controversies were considered to be those dealing with an attack on the trinitarian creeds or what Lutherans believed to be the "chief article" of faith derived from them (*BC* 292:1), namely "justified by faith apart from works prescribed by the law" (Rom. 3:28).

◇ ── ◇

Orthodoxy and Pietism

While Lutherans were establishing their confessional and territorial identity in Germany and Scandinavia, the royal house of England created an "Anglican Church" (from the Latin *anglia*, meaning "English") under Elizabeth I, which represented a middle course between Rome and Wittenberg. In Switzerland, the Reformation (later called "Reformed") combined Zwinglian and Calvinist elements with heavy emphasis on the latter. It made some inroads into Germany, but had its greatest impact in France, Holland, and Scotland.

After 1580, once Lutherans had agreed to subscribe to the normative confessions of faith contained in *The Book of Concord*, Lutheran princes enforced adherence to the confessions through territorial laws. Rulers sought uniform "orthodoxy" (from the Greek meaning "correct teaching") in their territories. Lutheran universities were instructed to teach "pure doctrine" and to develop effective polemics against both Catholics and Calvinists. The University of Wittenberg and, to a lesser degree, the University of Jena became the centers of Lutheran orthodox theology.

These institutions bred dogmatic theologians concerned with orthodox interpretations of confessional Lutheranism who produced heavy tomes dealing with various aspects of theology. Called *loci*, the various theological points were dealt with in a system of Aristotelian divisions of paragraphs and categories. Martin Chemnitz, for instance, wrote a voluminous *Examination of the Council of Trent* in which he refuted the Council point by point, accusing it of being unscriptural and totalitarian. Johann Gerhard, bishop of Koburg and professor at the University of Jena, produced nine volumes of Lutheran *Loci* that were viewed as the seventeenth century literary centerpiece of Lutheran orthodoxy. Abraham Calov, a Wittenberg professor, defended the literal inspiration of Holy Scripture, using it as a basis to condemn as heretical that which he did not consider Lutheran.

Calov's time was a time of Lutheran scholasticism, a rationalist drive using Aristotelian logic to establish eternal truths ranging from the literal inspiration of the Bible to specific ethical assertions derived from either the Bible or from the Lutheran Confessions. These scholastic theologians appealed to the authority of Luther, yet used Aristotelian means—even though Luther had been convinced that Aristotelian logic transformed Christian theology into a pagan philosophy.

Despite the political rulers' desire for uniformity in matters of faith and life, controversies between theologians and even between territories persisted. The University of Tübingen, for example, proposed a theory regarding God's incarnation, in which Jesus had *hidden* (from the Greek *krypsis*, meaning "hidden') his divine powers when he lived in Israel. The University of Giessen countered with its own theory based on the apostle Paul's declaration that Jesus "emptied himself" (*kenosis* in Greek), and had *relinquished* his divine powers. So "crypticists" fought "kenosists." Georg Calixtus, a professor at a university in Helmstedt, then attempted to mediate the dispute by demonstrating that during Christianity's first five centuries, both the human and the divine powers of Jesus were considered equally powerful. Thus, according to the "Calixtinians," there existed a "consensus of five centuries," affirmed especially in the trinitarian creeds, which spoke of Jesus as both human and divine. Calixtus was promptly opposed by some who called his position "syncretistic" (from the Greek *synkretismos*, meaning "something mixed"), alluding to his unorthodox mix of Christian and non Christian ways of thinking. Others called him a "crypto-Catholic."

The Thirty Years' War (1618–1648) interrupted many of these debates. There was widespread dissatisfaction with the Peace of Augsburg, which acknowledged only Catholics and adherents to the Augsburg Confession as legitimate expressions of Christianity. In 1608, Lutheran and Reformed princes had organized a joint military "union" to combat the Roman Catholic "league" led by the staunch Catholic Maximilian I of Bavaria. But the spark that caused the war was the rebellion of Bohemian princes against King Matthias of Bohemia (now Czechoslovakia), who had not kept his promise to grant toleration to Protestants. Most of Europe was soon involved in the Protestant and Catholic war.

The Protestant armies were routed by forces of the Catholic League in 1620. Eventually, King Gustavus Adolphus II of Sweden intervened on the Protestant side with a strong military force, thus saving Protestants from total defeat. He died in battle in 1632.

The Thirty Years' War devastated Europe and rearranged its political and religious map. People everywhere, especially in central Europe,

Gustavus Adolphus, King of Sweden

suffered immeasurable losses. At the war's end, almost one-third of the population had been decimated, some territories had changed rulers, and Switzerland and Holland had gained their independence and were acknowledged as independent countries. Emperor Ferdinand III finally ended the conflict by promising concessions to Protestants. Pope Innocent X sent out a papal bull protesting any concessions, but the papal bull no longer had the power it had at the time of Luther, and had no effect on the outcome.

The Peace of Westphalia in 1648 settled what had remained unsettled in 1555 with the Peace of Augsburg: except for the Hapsburg lands (Austria and some surrounding territories), each territory could adopt the religion of its ruler, as long as that religion was derived from a Lutheran, Reformed, or Anglican reformer. Groups like the Mennonites were not included in these provisions, but were, for the most part, tolerated.

The post-war years were filled with attempts to restore order and create greater tolerance. In Lutheran territories, many people, especially lay people, vented their frustrations against the oppressive orthodoxy imposed on them by their territorial princes and church leaders. Lay people complained that Lutheranism had become a "religion of the head" rather than a "religion of the heart." The latter appealed to them as a more attractive form of Christian life-style. They demanded better sermons than the arrogant and often ridiculous ramblings of orthodox pastors. One congregation, for example, had to listen to a sermon on Matthew 10:30 ("And even the hairs of your head are all counted") which the preacher subdivided into sections: the origins, style, and form of hair; its correct care; reminiscences, warnings, and comfort derived from hair; how to care for hair in good Christian fashion; and how to make use of it.

Philipp J. Spener (1635–1705), a pastor in Frankfurt/Main, led a revival movement dedicated to returning to the simplicity of the Christian Gospel and thus terminating the ineffective age of orthodoxy. A graduate of Strasbourg University, Spener was widely traveled and concerned about the low morale of the people. He began to cultivate a Lutheran piety and to hold meetings of small groups in his parsonage, calling them "assemblies of piety" *(collegia pietatis)*.

By 1675, Spener was ready to propose a program of renewal for the church. He published a small book entitled *Pious Desires (Pia Desideria)* (soon nicknamed the "Pietist Manifesto"), subtitled "Heartfelt Desire for a God-Pleasing Reform of the True Evangelical Church, Together with Several Simple Christian Proposals Looking Toward this End." He had already taught some of the basic ideas it contained in catechetical classes, and had emphasized the rite of confirmation, a rite little known among Lutherans but an effective ecclesiastical passage rite among the Reformed Swiss and French Calvinists.

In his "Pietist Manifesto," Spener, like Luther, first listed "corrupt conditions in the church": the amoral and bureaucratic behavior of political authorities, revealed by their lack of a Christian life-style; the equally amoral and bureaucratic behavior of the clergy, who cared more for themselves than for their flocks and were involved in useless controversies rather than paying attention to a truly Lutheran "practical theology"; and "defects of the common people" who had become "nominal Christians" indulging in drunkenness, lawsuits, and staying away from church services. Lutherans in Germany, Spener declared, had become an offense to other religions, including Judaism or Roman Catholicism, and needed to do a lot of penance before a radical rebirth of the kind of faith Luther taught and lived could again become a reality.

Spener proposed six remedies to what he considered the tragic situation of German Lutherans. They were: 1) make a more extensive use of the Word of God revealed in the Bible—more Bible study in small local groups consisting of clergy and laity; 2) revive what Luther had called the universal priesthood of all believers—less differentiation between clergy and laity; 3) place a greater emphasis on the practice rather than the merely rational knowledge of the Christian faith—more neighborly Christian love; 4) behave better when participating in controversies and ask for the help of prayer, penance, and Christian love—toning down polemics among the orthodox Lutherans; 5) improve the spiritual formation of future clergy in seminaries, the "seedbeds" (from the Latin *seminarium*) of personal piety—more practical theology and less academic theology; and 6) improve preaching so as to instill a practical piety in the congregation—more speaking and listening than mere ritual in worship services.

Spenerian Lutherans were soon dubbed "pietists" by their mostly orthodox opponents. The movement nevertheless became popular, and established an academic center in the newly founded University of Halle, where August H. Francke (1663–1727) taught an intensive program of education for mission at home and abroad.

Francke, one of Spener's disciples, was a great organizer blessed with the gift of persuasion. He founded orphanages for the child-victims of the war; started a Lutheran mission in Tranquebar, India, where his disciple Bartholomäus Ziegenbalg translated the New Testament into Hindi; and, assisted by Hildebrand von Canstein, a rich nobleman, created the first Lutheran Bible Society for the worldwide propagation of Scripture. He also established several schools which, by 1727, had a faculty of 170 who were educating twenty-two hundred children. The Prussian kings were so impressed by his efforts that they adopted his educational system for their public schools.

August Hermann Franke

Francke demanded a greater emotional investment from the laity than Spener had. Lay people were told to fight sin, break through to grace, and begin a born-again life at the expense of physical and/or psychological pleasures or joys. Dancing, partying, playing cards, and popular music were to be eschewed. More radical Pietists established small groups known as "conventicles" or "little churches within the big church" *(ecclesiola in ecclesia)* in and near Stuttgart in Württemberg. The Bible study movement in Stuttgart found a leader in the biblical scholar Johann A. Bengel, whose commentaries were widely used after 1742.

A particular form of German Lutheran pietism found expression in Herrnhurt (from the German, meaning "under the protection of the Lord"), a small town near Dresden and owned by Nikolaus von Zin-

Nikolaus Ludwig Graf von Zinzendorf   Hans Nielsen Hauge

zendorf (1700–1760). Zinzendorf, an Austrian count related to Saxon nobility, became attracted to Spener and his ideas. He was a typical baroque figure: he was cosmopolitan, widely traveled, and in many respects peculiar. For a time he talked of "sifting," or looking for new ways to express his Christian feelings and commitments, during which he attended German theological schools.

In 1727, Zinzendorf granted a group of Czech Protestants permission to settle in Herrnhut. These refugees were Moravian Brethren, disciples of the Prague reformer Jan Hus who had been burned at the stake in 1415. Moravians had since become pacifists and were committed to an intensive, pious community life and to a Christian unity made visible by the ancient tradition of having bishops in apostolic succession. Zinzendorf, who was deeply involved in the Herrnhut community, was seen as something of a father figure there. He was consecrated bishop of the Moravian Brethren in 1737 in Berlin by the Reformed Court Preacher Daniel E. Jablonski, who claimed to be in apostolic succession with all other Christian bishops. Through his consecration, Zinzendorf established a link between Lutheranism and a historical Protestant episcopate. The Moravian Brethren in turn subscribed to the unaltered Augsburg Confession of 1530 and were accepted in Saxony as legitimate Lutherans.

Zinzendorf, who was a rather autocratic ruler, used some peculiar theological language—the Trinity was "Papa, Mama, and the Little

Lamb"—and initiated some peculiar customs, like creating a "Mustard Seed Order" to symbolize fast-growing faith. He nevertheless had great influence on Pietist Lutheranism, especially in his travels throughout the United States (some regard him as the patriarch of American Lutheranism) and in his influence on John Wesley, the Methodist leader in England. Spener, Francke, and Zinzendorf made Pietism an integral part of Lutheranism.

In Scandinavia, Hans Nielsen Hauge (1771–1824) became an ardent disciple of Spener and Pietism. He violated Norwegian law by preaching in the streets and by holding assemblies outside the official church buildings, spending time in jail (1804–11 and 1814–16). He used his time in jail to write books and treatises about the Christian way of engaging in business and politics. Hauge remained loyal to the Norwegian Lutheran state church, even though some of his disciples wanted to break away. Haugean Pietism remained a substantial force in Scandinavian Lutheranism.

In Finland, many people were spiritually awakened by a Lutheran peasant named Paavo Ruotsalainen (1777–1852). He claimed to have had spiritual experiences similar to those of Luther, and he inspired many people with his powerful personality and simple, strong piety which, though similar to Pietism, had not been shaped by it.

In Sweden, Pastor Lars Levy Laestadius (1800–1861), known as "the Reviver of the North," continued to fuel the popular Pietism that was prevalent in Germany and Scandinavia by preaching about the need to be forgiven and to begin a new life with God. He and the other Lutheran Pietists considered themselves disciples of Luther and advocates of Luther's reforms, now no longer confined to Roman Catholicism but extended to a Lutheranism that had become stale and apathetic.

◇——————————————————————————————◇

The Impact of Enlightenment Philosophy

The Peace of Westphalia in 1648 and the Toleration Act in England in 1689 signaled the end of political religious bias and the beginning of religious liberty. The loss of ecclesiastical power was accompanied by an intellectual "Age of Enlightenment" concentrating on the earthly

life rather than the afterlife. Beginning with René Descartes (1596–
1650), known for his slogan "I think, therefore I am," philosophers
focused on free reason, the goodness of both human and non-human
nature, and on God as a distant deity, who, as a kind of clock maker,
had created the universe to run of itself. Not even the creator of that
universe could alter its laws.

English members of the enlightenment, such as David Hume (1711–
76), called themselves "deists" or "free thinkers" and defended a "natural" or "civil" religion grounded in toleration of all religions. The
French philosopher Voltaire (1694–1778) distinguished between the clergy's religion, marked by the arrogance of power, and a generalized
religiosity that ignored doctrines, particularly the doctrine of immortality. Jean-Jaques Rousseau (1712–78) aimed to unify humankind by
devising a system of social contracts based on reason, with a strong
commitment to nature, which constituted the world of feelings and
emotions. Frederick II, the Prussian king who ruled from 1740–86,
embraced the new Enlightenment philosophy and decreed that everyone
might be saved from sin by whatever means he or she found helpful.

Lutherans, especially theologians, adapted in various ways to the
new way of thinking. Some elevated the study of history to the throne
of "theological science." Johann G. Walch, for example, did so with an
edition of Luther's works, and in 1755 Johann von Mosheim published
an "objective" scientific history of institutional Christianity. Others,
desiring to be "rational" in their assessment of Christian origins, made
judgments like that of Hermann S. Reimarus (1694–1768), who claimed
that Jesus' disciples had invented Jesus' resurrection and had stolen his
corpse from the tomb. Nominally Lutheran, most of these defenders of
the Enlightenment had little, if any, connection with the institutional
church. The German philosopher Immanuel Kant summed up this new
way of thinking in a popular treatise, published in 1784, entitled "What
is Enlightenment?" His answer: "Enlightenment is the change from
immaturity to maturity; and maturity is the ability to use one's mind
without being led by another mind." Kantians thought going to church
was being immature, unenlightened, and, indeed superstitious.

The most influential theologian after the Enlightenment was Friedrich Schleiermacher (1768–1834), who tried to combine the rationalism
of Enlightenment philosophy with a theology based on pious experience.
He intended to attract intellectuals who favored rationalist principles,

Immanuel Kant   Friedrich Schleiermacher

"the cultured despisers of Christianity." Everyone is religious, he contended, and it is with awe that everyone senses a divine power. This
awe is expressed in a "feeling" *(Gefühl)* of dependence on a God who
is greater than any power known on earth.

Schleiermacher's influence on Lutherans was powerful even though
he was a Reformed theologian. He appealed to Pietists by declaring
that religion is a sense and taste of the infinite, which precedes dogma,
ritual, and ethics. But he also appealed to the orthodox because of his
rational exposition of the Christian faith as centered in Christ. He
declared that believers must live in the same consciousness of God that
is so dramatically portrayed in the Gospel of John. This Christocentric
consciousness is incorporated in the church, which is a living community
nurtured by the Holy Spirit rather than just an institution.

Schleiermacher's claim of the existence of an innate religiosity tran-
scended the views of opposing parties in Lutheranism. He was quite
"liberal" in the sense that he expanded biblical and trinitarian notions
to include the mysterious arena of romantic-mystical human experience.
Thus rationalism and pietism could be united in what Kantian philosophers called "phenomenology": external facts of which the ultimate
meaning remains a mystery; a "postulation," an assumption of freedom,
God, and immortality. As a result, Schleiermacher's disciples could, with

Georg W. F. Hegel

Kant, assert that one lives with the stars above and with a moral consciousness within oneself—both being beyond rational explanation.

Lutherans in Germany and Scandinavia remained solidly anchored either in a confessional orthodoxy or in an individualistic pietism. Most pastors taught either "pure doctrine" or propagated the conversion of the individual to a more obviously Christian life by way of a "rebirth." Professors at the University of Halle, the great center of German pietism, shaped many of their graduates by combining the various ways of thinking with a typically Lutheran piety that centered on justification by faith and was manifested in a sanctified life-style. To be born again meant more than being a free thinker.

Sometimes a romantic spirit of discovery even led Lutherans back to a study of the Bible and the Lutheran Confessions in *The Book of Concord.* Some called themselves "neo-orthodox" since they had recommitted themselves to the Augsburg Confession with a romanticism regarding the past that had emerged in intellectual circles in Berlin.

Some Lutherans became "neo-Lutherans" by affirming both a confessional orthodoxy and an ethical pietism to demonstrate that pure doctrine leads to a pure life-style.

But opposites attract. Georg W. F. Hegel (1770–1831) viewed all of world history as a synthesis of a thesis and an antithesis. Some Lutherans, taking their cue from Hegel, considered the merging of Lutheran orthodoxy and pietism an inevitable historical synthesis of two originally opposite traditions. This new synthesis was dubbed the "age of awakening," manifested in a revival of Lutheran confessionalism and a promotion of Lutheran pietism.

Old World Network

--- ◇ ---

Contexts

By 1817, the tercentenary of Luther's reformation, European Lutheranism was confronted by changes in all aspects of life. Technological advances, such as the invention of the locomotive in 1814, enabled improvements in communications and commerce. In 1818, the steamship linked England and the United States and made transatlantic crossings much shorter. The telegraph revolutionized communications, and other technological advances like the telephone, electric lighting, and radio soon followed.

People referred to this period as the "industrial revolution," for machinery was being invented to speed up the manufacture of goods and to create more factories. In England, these inventions created a powerful fourth estate alongside the nobility, the clergy, and the burghers—the blue-collar worker. All aspects of business and trade were changed by goods mass-produced with cheap labor, especially that of women and children. The difference between the very poor and the rich grew wider.

Adam Smith (1723–90) and his disciples formulated economic theories in support of the industrial revolution, culminating in the notion of competition between national economies, which were later known as the "free market system." Nations started to compete with each other in the production and export of goods, and established customs regulations to control imports. National capitalism predominated.

The age of Enlightenment had declared human reason the highest authority. As a result, forms of government based on hereditary rule now came under question. Other forms, such as democracies and republics, were being advocated and tested. The American Declaration of Independence of 1776 claimed the egalitarian right to individual liberty, and the ensuing revolution established a republic. The French Revolution of 1789 virtually worshiped human reason as the instrument of government and fought to establish a democracy.

The rise of Napoleon in France brought Europe to the brink of political collapse. When he was finally defeated, the victorious powers which met at the Congress of Vienna in 1815 affirmed the great monarchies of England, Prussia, Austria, and Russia as guardians of the peace in an effort to prevent radical political changes. A "holy alliance" between Austria, Prussia and Russia was formed to enforce the decisions arrived at by military force.

The followers of Karl Marx (1818–83), calling themselves Socialists and Communists, advocated abolishing monarchies in favor of the rule of the common people. But their revolution, staged in 1848 in France and Germany, was unsuccessful. The old order prevailed.

Church and state began to move further apart as politicians of various stripes demanded the separation of both realms. In 1787, the delegates to the Continental Congress in America included in the American Constitution an article on the total separation of church and state.

Nineteenth-century philosophers experimented with ideas and theories. Some even announced the end of Christianity; others merely ignored it. Friedrich Nietzsche (1844–1900), an influential philosopher and the son of a Lutheran pastor, declared that God was dead, calling for a transformation of Christian values. The French scholar Alphonse de Gobineau developed a theory in 1853 that classified and evaluated human "races." He invented the term "Aryan," which identified a blond, blue-eyed Nordic super-race; he also classified Jews as the lowest race and stated that they should be eliminated. (Both these ideas were later embraced by the Nazis in Germany.) Richard Wagner (1813–83) adapted ancient German myths in his operas to celebrate the German "master

Friedrich Nietzsche

race." British scientist Charles Darwin (1809–82) developed a theory on the origins of species, concluding that species of animals evolved from others, and that humankind had evolved from apes. Much of what at first seemed odd and extravagant later became commonly accepted worldwide.

Lutherans watched with apprehension the growing popularity of Roman Catholicism. Rome rejected Enlightenment philosophy, labeling it a rebirth of paganism. Catholic thinking was still dominated by medieval theology, based on the ideas of Thomas Aquinas (1225–74). The Catholic Counter-Reformation had been quite successful, especially in Austria and southern Germany. Lutherans lived with the bitter memory of the 1732 expulsion of thirty thousand Lutherans from Salzburg by a capricious archbishop. Rome had helped Belgium gain independence from Holland in 1830, and Italy and Spain remained Catholic bulwarks against Protestantism. Only in Austria did the spirit of the Enlightenment favor Lutherans, when in 1781 the Catholic king Joseph II granted them and the Calvinists religious toleration.

Lutherans observed with great misgivings the Catholics' increasing devotion to Mary, although they themselves accepted her as the "mother of God." Rome's institution in 1854 of the dogma of Mary's immaculate conception convinced Lutherans that worship of Jesus Christ was being endangered by the cult of Mary.

Another cause of apprehension was the pope's increasing power and influence. When the dogma of papal infallibility was declared at the First Vatican Council in 1870, Lutherans were deeply offended. They also feared the increasing number of political agreements between Rome and some governments, such as its "concordat" with Napoleon in 1801. In 1872, when Prince Otto von Bismarck proposed legislation to limit Catholic influence in Germany, Rome mustered sufficient popular support to defeat it. Three centuries after Luther's reformation, Catholicism was still a formidable opponent of Lutheranism in Martin Luther's homeland.

In Denmark, however, Lutheranism had been the state religion since 1665. The king was the head of the church, and Lutheran pastors and bishops were servants of the state. All church policy was established through negotiations with the government.

Norway, a part of Denmark until 1814, and then a part of Sweden until it attained independence in 1905, nurtured its own Lutheran leadership with the help of the University of Oslo.

Lutheranism became the state religion of Sweden in 1593, when it accepted the three ecumenical creeds and the Augsburg Confession as official confessions.

Finland, annexed by Russia in 1809, received Russian concessions and allowed Lutherans their religious liberty as long as they did not oppose the government.

Prussian Lutherans faced a severe crisis when King Frederick William III, quite enamored of Enlightenment philosophy, proposed the merger of Lutheran and Reformed churches in order to consolidate his power as "supreme bishop" of the territory. A royal commission was to bring the merger about in 1817 as a fitting memorial to Luther's Ninety-Five Theses of 1517. After a short but bitter struggle, both the Lutherans and the Reformed strongly rejected the merger, and the king withdrew his proposal.

The king's defeat with regard to the merger prompted some Lutherans to call for a new Lutheran commitment to the Lutheran Confessions. On October 31, 1817, Pastor Klaus Harms, the most popular preacher in Northern Germany, published his own Ninety-Five Theses in Kiel. The Theses called for loyalty to Luther, to the Augsburg Confession, and to a Prussian Lutheranism cleansed of all Reformed and Calvinistic elements. Harms found additional support in Bavaria, where the Bavarian pastor Wilhelm Löhe was initiating a confessional and liturgical revival. This conservative movement was solidified in 1830, the tercentenary of the Augsburg Confession, and in 1841 the Prussian Lutheran conservatives organized the "Evangelical Lutheran Church in Prussia."

◇————————————————————————————◇

Theologies

Many theological trends and schools in nineteenth-century Germany and Scandinavia influenced Lutheran intellectual life. Theologians defined the sources of Lutheran thought and life in terms of the power of personal religious experience, historical development, and biblical-confessional norms.

The "Tübingen School" stressed historical criticism and historical development. David F. Strauss (1808–74) initiated a long controversy with the publication of his biography of Jesus. He distinguished between "the Christ of faith" and "the Jesus of history." It is difficult to distinguish the one from the other because the Bible's language is clothed in myths. Thus no historical truth can safely be established. Christ, he said, was "manufactured" by believers who make dogmatic claims, such as the resurrection, without convincing evidence; therefore Jesus Christ, the very source of Christianity, cannot be trusted scientifically. Strauss contended that Christianity has no more power to convince than atheism

David F. Strauss

has. Basing his argument on the inconclusiveness of biblical evidence, Ludwig Feuerbach (1804–72) concluded that all theology is anthropology, in other words, that God is the result of human projection divinizing an idea of something absolute and calling it "god."

The Tübingen church historian Ferdinand C. Baur (1792–1860) attempted to demonstrate how seemingly contradictory developments in the history of Christianity are held together by basic dogmatic convictions grounded in the doctrine of God's incarnation in Jesus and in the doctrine of God's reconciliation with sinful creatures. Albrecht Ritschl (1822–89), one of Baur's Lutheran disciples who taught in Berlin, used a dialectical method to demonstrate the power of the Christian faith; he said that Christianity is grounded in God's incarnation in Jesus and in the dogma of the Trinity, which are the two fundamental pillars that have endured throughout time. Both point to a universal Christian morality evident in the teachings of Jesus, who will usher in the "kingdom of God." It is an "objective" reality guaranteed by dogma, and it is a "subjective" reality experienced in moral action. Christianity exists in the dialectic of both these realities.

The "Erlangen school" defended Lutheran orthodoxy on the basis of the inspiration of the Bible and the Lutheran Confessions. An important voice of the Erlangen school was that of Johannes Konrad von Hofmann (1810–77), who defended the traditional medieval and Reformation notion of "salvation history." This notion asserts that the Bible reveals a process of promise and fulfillment which is disclosed in the testimony of faithful readers who are born again when they encounter Scripture. To be born again means to be converted to total faith in God, incarnate in Jesus, who justifies the ungodly.

Adolph G. Harless, another Erlanger, declared that all theological reflection is based on the "rebirth" one experiences as the result of divine grace, and that this creates a new, moral Christian community. Holy Scripture and the Lutheran Confessions were to him the most important testimonies to the power of God's word, which transforms people into beings morally bound to God in Christ alone. Erlangen theologians soon gained the powerful support of governments that feared liberal theologies which reflected the revolutionary spirit of 1848; it embraced a radical secularization and socialist/communist/materialistic ideas.

Lutheran theologies in Scandinavia were as varied as those in Germany. The most influential theologian was the Dane Nikolai Grundtvig (1783–1872), who viewed Christianity as a "cultic drama" grounded in the liturgy of word and sacrament, and asserted that the institutional church and its history were the "proof" of Christian truth. He saw all of Christian life permeated by "rebirth": the gospel re-humanizes people and makes them brothers and sisters, and the church is the true home of humanity. Grundtvig had great influence on the Danish people, whom he tried to draw into a system of Christian education through public schools. Many admired his preaching and teaching style, as well as his work as a composer of hymns like "Built on a Rock the Church Shall Stand Even When Steeples Are Falling."

Grundtvig and his programs were sharply criticized by the theologian and philosopher Søren Kierkegaard (1813–55), who criticized the institutional church for compromising the radicalness of the Christian faith. According to Kierkegaard, the life of faith is always "exceptional existence" in the world, characterized by "fear and trembling" and the experiencing of the "paradox" illustrated in the story of Abraham sac-

N. F. S. Grundtvig

rificing Isaac (Gen. 22). In treatises, books, and journals, Kierkegaard described what he called the true initiation into Christianity by way of a "borderline existence" always close to the abyss. Every Christian must face the abyss, Kierkegaard argued, just as he himself had faced it when he broke his engagement to Regina Olsen in 1840. Consequently, humanity suffers from a spiritual "sickness unto death" that had overwhelmed the Danish church and its pompous ritual. Kierkegaard left the church in 1854, accusing its leaders of being fraudulent hypocrites.

Norwegian theologians, on the other hand, criticized Grundtvig for stressing tradition, manifested in his sacramentalism, more than Scripture. In the 1850s, members of the faculty of the University of Oslo joined Haugean Pietists in attacking Grundtvigianism. Some favored Kierkegaard. Candidates for the ordained ministry were often judged on the basis of whether or not they followed the "Grundtvigian heresy."

Søren Kierkegaard   Karl Rosenius

Some Swedish theologians supported a high liturgy and confessional theology in Lund in the 1850s. They focused on the church, viewing the office of the ordained ministry as God-willed. This High Church movement was accompanied by a Bible and tract movement led by the Lund pastor Henrik Schartau (1757–1825). Schartau was a Pietist but later moved toward a greater appreciation of the Lutheran Confessions. Many pastors imitated his "father-children" model in their relations with their congregations.

Methodist migrant preachers from England frequently appeared in Lutheran congregations and injected a concern for foreign mission. Karl O. Rosenius (1816–68), a Lutheran layman and son of a pastor, collaborated with the British Methodist preacher George Scott and founded a street mission in Stockholm. Their missionary program was disseminated in their journal *Pietists* and in a "Mission Paper" in 1834. The result was the founding of a variety of mission organizations and prayer meetings. But Rosenius rejected Pietist legalism and moralism, and instead advocated the "sweet gospel" of love.

The Swedish government was unsuccessful in its attempts to stop the increasing power of the laity. In 1860, laws were passed that allowed people to leave the state church to join the "free churches," which had less restrictive polity and greater emotional piety.

◇——————————————————————————◇

Church, State, and Witness

Lutherans in Germany still faced a struggle with territorial governments attempting to create union churches. The merger of Lutherans and Reformed was avoided in Prussia, but union churches were created in other territories: in 1817 in the Dukedom of Nassau, in the Palatinate in 1818, in Baden in 1821, in Rhine-Hesse in 1822, and in smaller territories at about the same time.

The Prussian king still sought a compromise, and in 1822 proposed a new *Service Book and Hymnal* (called *Agende* in German), causing a literary and political quarrel which finally ended in 1829, when he permitted the printing of provincial *Agenden* as alternatives to the one he had proposed. This meant that Lutherans could retain a purely Lutheran order of worship in provinces where they were dominant. In Silesia, however, Lutherans rejected all compromises, resulting in the jailing of a pastor in 1834 and the emigration of Lutherans to North America and Australia.

Prussian Lutherans, influenced by the diplomacy of the well-known Duke Otto von Bismarck, eventually agreed to a common polity. A new constitution, drawn up in 1876, centered on four provisions: 1) the establishment of a parish council responsible for directing the work of the local congregation; 2) the convening of an annual district synod meeting to coordinate the work of local congregations; 3) the establishment of a provincial synod, to meet every third year; and 4) the establishment of a general synod, headed by a synod council, to meet every sixth year. New hymnals, containing streamlined forms of worship, accompanied these organizational reforms.

Lutheran Pietists continued to be concerned for personal piety and mission. At times, they were supported by orthodox Lutherans like Wilhelm Löhe. Löhe had encountered poverty in the villages of Bavaria and sought to relieve it by way of schools and the establishment of deaconess communities. He also helped emigrants.

PASTOR WILLIAM LOEHE,
Born 1808, died 1872.

William Löhe

Johann H. Wichern

The continuing concern for "practical Christianity" created the "inner mission" movement in Germany. Johann H. Wichern (1808–81), a Lutheran pastor, became quite concerned about the social conditions existing in Hamburg. In 1833, he began to gather starving children and established an orphanage known as the "rough house," which soon became a model for the nurture of neglected and abused children, especially teenagers. In 1842, Wichern pushed for an "inner mission" that would care for the social outcasts, the poor, the homeless, and especially the neglected children. He laid out his plan for a mission in Germany at the first national *Kirchentag* (1848), the national assembly of churches, calling for social change in the name of Christ rather than in the name of Karl Marx. In 1856, he was appointed to organize such a mission, with the assistance of the Department for Domestic Affairs. Wichern, in many tracts and sermons, stressed the positive roles of family, church, and state in the foundation of a healthy national life. His work toward attaining healthy national life became one of the resources Germany employed in organizing its modern welfare system.

After 1881, the inner mission was directed by Pastor Friedrich Bodelschwingh (1831–1910). Plagued by doubts of God's love, Bod-

The "Rough House" at Horn, Germany

elschwingh had committed himself to the care of the poor, first among unemployed laborers in Paris, then in Rhineland-Westphalia. In 1876, he was called to head "Bethel," a house of deaconesses and an institution for epileptic patients. In the inner mission, he founded a series of ecclesiastical welfare organizations and programs which eventually affected all levels of society, either as sponsors or as recipients of aid. He cared particularly for the "brothers in the street," who were unemployed migrating laborers, and for whom he founded a string of homes called "colonies."

Married, and deeply troubled by the deaths of four children within two weeks, Bodelschwingh talked about the difficult relationship between God and His children on earth. He declared "the word 'incurable' should not be found in the dictionary of a Christian." He was convinced that helping the outcasts, especially the homeless, provided an opportunity to obey the will of God.

Bodelschwingh wanted to create a clergy willing to deal with misery and poverty in the cities, contending that the sick and the poor are the best teachers of candidates for ministry. He also said that foreign and domestic missions ought to become one, based on his conviction (later inscribed on his tombstone) that "since it is by God's mercy that we are engaged in this ministry, we do not lose heart" (2 Cor. 4:1).

Friedrich Bodelschwingh   Gertrude Reichardt, the first deaconess

On the whole, nineteenth century Lutheranism reflected the general situation of Protestants in Europe. Methodism in England engaged in massive programs of social and missionary work. Reformed churches in Switzerland advocated programs of foreign mission and established the famous "Basel Mission" in 1815. Dutch Reformed churches in Holland followed suit. A Lutheran church in France shared rights and privileges with the Reformed and Roman Catholic churches after 1802, and the theological faculty in Strassbourg became the center of French Lutheran theology. Lutherans in Hungary received equal rights in 1833, and Austria granted them toleration in 1861. In Poland and Russia, Lutherans did not fare as well, but continued to survive with the aid of Baltic Lutherans. Some Lutherans in Russia suffered persecution because of their German heritage. German Lutheranism was quite committed to an extensive missionary witness abroad, especially through mission societies. These included, most notably, the Berlin Society (1824), the Rhenish Society (1828), and the Leipzig Society (1819).

Lutheranism, however, did not attract many people in Germany or Scandinavia. Despite constitutional, ecclesiastical, liturgical, and ethical attempts to reform the church, many Lutherans shied away from active involvement in the church.

Deaconess House at Kaiserswerth

The emigrants' farewell to native land

New World Immigrants

◇

Sailing to North America

Lutherans first settled in North America in the Dutch territory known as "New Netherlands" along the Hudson River and in "New Sweden" along the Delaware River. Most came from Germany and Scandinavia, and a few from Poland, and established small settlements during the 1640s. Many Germans arrived from the Rhine Valley at the end of the Thirty Years' War in 1648, founding Germantown, near Philadelphia, and settling in other communities along the banks of the Susquehanna River in Pennsylvania, where the Quaker William Penn's liberal laws proved hospitable to other religions. Some went south to settle in North Carolina around New Bern. By 1690, there were about one thousand German and Scandinavian Lutherans living in Wilmington and along the Delaware River. Soon German settlers outnumbered the Dutch and the Swedes on the Atlantic seaboard.

Romantic notions about North America spurred immigration. Lutherans left Europe in increasing numbers, despite the warnings of earlier settlers that "roasted pigs won't fly into your mouth." Immigration meant six to eight weeks of ocean travel with disease and rough conditions, but immigrants kept coming. Over sixty-five thousand Germans entered the port of Philadelphia between 1727 and 1775; most of them settled in Pennsylvania, Maryland and Virginia, though some continued on to North Carolina. In 1734, about three hundred of the thirty thousand Austrian Lutherans who had been driven out of Salzburg by the Salzburg bishop established the Ebenezer settlement on the banks of the Savannah River in Georgia. The first Lutherans appeared in New England and Nova Scotia in the 1760s.

"White servitude" paved the way to the longed-for better life for many Lutheran immigrants. The majority of German immigrants sold themselves as indentured servants to sponsors in the New World to pay for their passage, and were known as "redemptionists," since they worked as slaves until they redeemed their passage money.

There were few, if any, pastors who led the early settlers. Jacob Fabritius, a native Silesian hailing from Hungary, was the first pastor to establish a Lutheran congregation in New York. However, he soon lost his members because of his bad language and heavy drinking. Sweden granted some pastors permission to organize Lutheran assemblies in Delaware. In the 1750s, Sweden commissioned twenty-five pastors to sail to the Delaware River colony. Andrew Rudman, who had been trained by the German Pietists in Halle, was one of these pastors. He ordained Justus Falckner to organize the Lutherans along the Hudson River, since there were enough German Lutherans in Manhattan by 1742 to request German worship services. By 1776 the Swedish pastors established Swedish and English speaking congregations in Delaware.

The principal source of information about Lutheran emigration was the Pietist headquarters in Halle, which published a magazine called "Halle Reports" to spread the news, and which trained pastors for duty in the American colonies. They sent a young pastor named Henry M. Muhlenberg to North America to unite Lutherans in America, but "vagabond preachers" and "pretenders" made his task difficult.

In 1748, Muhlenberg managed to organize the "Ministerium of North America," which was the seed bed for an organized church, and first consisted of six pastors and a number of lay delegates, most of them from Pennsylvania. The Ministerium elected a "superintendent" (from the Latin for "bishop") and a president in 1750. By 1781 there was a constitution providing for districts and, eventually, for synods modeled after the Dutch Reformed polity. Muhlenberg called this new

Henry M. Muhlenberg

church "a church still needing to be planted" *(ecclesia plantanda)*, know-ing that it was a term that would be well understood by the Lutheran farmers dominating the church.

The new Lutheran church in America began to erect log church buildings, sometimes financed by both Lutheran and Reformed mem-bers. Conditions had yoked them together as Protestants from Europe in contradistinction to Anglicans, Roman Catholics, and "sects." Dis-agreements and controversies over language arose between the Dutch Reformed and the Germans, but Muhlenberg, dividing his time between New York and Pennsylvania, managed to re-establish peace between them. A part of the Lutheran immigrant luggage included the conti-nental controversies between the "orthodoxists" (strict adherents to the Lutheran Confessions) and the Pietists, who stressed the born-again experience over "pure doctrine." Muhlenberg liked to say that the "or-thodoxists" tried to adhere to the unaltered Augsburg Confession "with unaltered hearts."

As a result of these differences, worship services among the early Lutherans in North America were simplified and were closer to the

Reformed than to the Catholics. Swedes still clung to chanting and organ music, but Germans tended to do without these "Catholic" features. Sermons were long, and Holy Communion was rare, usually only once or twice a year. There was a strong commitment to Sunday School education, but very little interest in mission to Native Americans or blacks. Generally, Lutherans tolerated slavery.

Since Episcopalians and Methodists were organizing themselves, Lutherans did not want to lag behind. The Pennsylvania Ministerium became a model for other groups of Lutherans. Others were cutting their ties to Europe, but Lutherans did not, and the Pietist connection remained a strong one, providing them with ammunition to combat new and dangerous philosophies like Deism. Many of the political founders of the United States, such as Thomas Jefferson, were Deists. They adhered to a broadly moral, "civil" religion, and believed in an impersonal deity who ran the world by laws that could be discerned by reason.

◇──────────────────────────────◇

The Problem of Assimilation

Increasing migration to the South and the West made it more difficult for German and Scandinavian Lutherans to maintain contact with their homelands. By 1817 there were more than 650 Lutheran congregations in the United States, some of them south and west of the Missouri River; also, synods were being organized in Ohio, Virginia, and North Carolina. Lutherans were confronted with different ideas and different religions, such as revivalism. Some circuit-riding Lutheran pastors sometimes held camp meetings, but German and Scandinavian minds never really warmed up to such rituals.

The most influential pastors favored what they called "American Evangelicalism," as John G. Schmucker did, and desired a union of all religious parties, provided they adhered to Scripture and rejected "infidelity." Most Lutherans, however, though quite willing to associate with the Reformed and the Moravians, shied away from close contact with other religious groups. In 1817, on the three-hundredth anniversary of the Reformation, Lutheran leaders called for a revival of Luther's ideas and for the principles of Luther's Reformation to be the foundation of pastors' education. They opened a second small academy in New York (the first, called Hartwick, had been opened in 1815 in Oneonta, New York) which stressed the teaching of Luther's Catechisms and traditional Lutheran hymns and liturgy.

Some Lutherans in Germany were such strong adherents to the unaltered Augsburg Confession that they fled Germany rather than obey the proposed merger with the Reformed, advocated by the Prussian government in 1817. Johannes A. Grabau, a Pietist pastor from Halle who had been imprisoned in Prussia, led about one thousand Lutherans to settle in Buffalo, New York. Others migrated to Wisconsin and were joined by Lutherans from Saxony. Pastor Martin Stephan was elected their bishop and then led about seven hundred from Wisconsin to St. Louis, where he helped found the Missouri Synod in 1847. Missouri Synod Lutherans would become known as the strongest adherents to the Lutheran Confessions, refusing to make any adjustments in the New World. They trained their future pastors in St. Louis at Concordia Seminary, founded in 1844, and refused to compromise their confessional position. In the East, the conservative Lutherans battled other Lutherans, especially in the Buffalo Synod, over issues of loyalty to the Lutheran Confessions. The Buffalo Synod was dissolved in 1877, and the conservatives joined the Wisconsin Synod.

The leading Lutheran pastor and theologian at the beginning of the nineteenth century was Samuel S. Schmucker (1799–1873). Educated at the University of Pennsylvania and Princeton Theological Seminary, Schmucker longed to provide Lutherans with a solid organization, a systematic theology, and a seminary that would teach future Lutheran pastors. His dream was realized when the General Synod established a seminary in Gettysburg, Pennsylvania in 1826, and appointed Schmucker professor and president of the seminary. Future pastors attended seminary for three years before being sent out into parishes. Gettysburg College was founded in 1832 to provide future seminarians with a classical education resembling the European model.

Schmucker considered himself a confessional Lutheran trying to adapt European Lutheranism to American conditions. He translated German theological works and taught his students his own version of what he entitled "Popular Theology." In his view, the Augsburg Confession was the heart of theological education and Lutheran life.

Samuel S. Schmucker

Schmucker and a few others rejected slavery (Schmucker's house was even a station of the "underground railroad" which helped slaves escape), but they had little success in persuading most Lutherans to agree with them.

Controversies among Lutherans continued. They argued over whether to have worship services in German or in English, about the meaning of faithfulness to the Lutheran Confessions, how to relate to other religious groups and other experiences, and whether or not to tolerate slavery. Many Lutherans had become accustomed to revivalist ways, such as being converted through fear of God's punishment. They instituted the practice of having future converts sit on the "mourner's bench," usually right in front of the church, in order to be visible to those already converted when they went in to worship, and preachers would talk about them and their sins during the service. Schmucker

Gettysburg Seminary

and other Lutheran leaders disagreed with this practice, although they favored Sunday "blue laws" prohibiting drinking, dancing, and other forms of entertainment.

Germans, Danes, Norwegians, Swedes, and Finns had become well organized in the nineteenth century, but there was not much contact between them. Synods were formed along ethnic lines, and some were even known by the name of their leader, such as the "Eielsen Synod," named after the Norwegian itinerant lay preacher Elling Eielsen, or the "Hauge Synod" named after the Pietist lay theologian Hans N. Hauge. Some Lutherans began to complain that the church, organized in this way, had lost its original purpose to be a missionary force in the world. The Pennsylvania Ministerium even sent its own missionary abroad; John F. Heyer joined German Pietists and Moravians in India in 1841. An American Luther Society was organized in 1859 and began printing Luther's works in English, beginning with a thirty volume edition published in 1876.

Some Lutherans were more concerned for social welfare in a land with a fast-growing population suffering hardship and having problems assimilating. William A. Passavant worked to establish an "inner mission" program modeled after the German Pietist programs. In 1849, he founded the first Protestant hospital in Pittsburgh, and he supported the institution of a deaconess movement sponsored by German Pietists.

Tensions within the organization increased over the issue of how to adjust European Lutheranism to life in the New World. "Neo-Lutherans" wanted to have closer ties with Methodists and Puritans in order to build a united front against Catholics, theologically confused revivalists, and infidels. "Old Lutherans," represented by the Missouri and Wisconsin Synods, wanted to maintain strict loyalty to the Lutheran Confessions and ties to Germany and Scandinavia. Schmucker and other east coast Lutherans favored a compromise between confessionalism and Americanism.

The first violent controversy in the General Synod was caused by the publication in 1855 of Schmucker's "American Recension of the Augsburg Confession" in the *Definite Synodical Platform*. The Recension asserted that the Augsburg Confession contained five "errors" that could not be tolerated by the heirs of the Reformation and should be dropped. They were: 1) continuing the celebration of the Mass; 2) using private confession; 3) rejecting the Sabbath (blue) law on Sundays; 4) affirming baptismal regeneration; and 5) teaching the real, bodily presence of Christ in the Eucharist. A war of pamphlets and hectic debates ensued, after which only three small synods—East Ohio, Wittenberg, and Olive Branch—sided with Schmucker. The other synods, even the Pennsylvania Ministerium, rejected Schmucker's radical reform program.

But the controversy was far from over. Tracts and pamphlets appeared, arguing for or against Schmucker's "American Lutheranism." Finally, sixty-four pastors and lay people held a meeting to debate both sides of the issue. They finally agreed to subscribe to the norms set by the General Synod which was "absolute assent" to the Word of God and "fundamental agreement with the Augsburg Confession."

Schmucker agreed with the statement but reserved the right to answer further criticism. By 1864, however, he had grown tired of the controversy and resigned as president and professor at the seminary, and was succeeded by James A. Brown. Hostilities flared up again, since Brown was Schmucker's worst critic. Schmucker opponents lobbied the Pennsylvania Ministerium for a new seminary. It was founded in 1864 in Philadelphia and was committed to the preservation of loyalty to the Augsburg Confession and to the Lutheran liturgical tradition.

C. F. W. Walther, a leading Missouri Synod theologian, proposed holding "free conferences" to reestablish Lutheran unity. Four confer

William A. Passavant   Carl F. W. Walther

ences were held between 1856 and 1859, but did not attain the desired unity. A "General Lutheran Council" was organized in 1867, with thirteen synods as members, but was more of a service agency for a federation of synods than a strong voice for Lutheran unity. Succumbing to pressure to stay away from ecumenism, it reserved "Lutheran pulpits for Lutheran ministers only." This 1872 stipulation was reaffirmed in 1875 and became known as the Galesburg Rule.

The American Civil War divided Lutherans along with the nation. Southern Lutherans organized in support of slavery and the Confederacy, and isolated themselves from Northern Lutherans, most of whom also did not oppose slavery. This kind of division only impeded the progress of assimilation, increased immigration, and helped maintain ties to Europe.

By 1880, Lutherans could be found in California, Oregon, Washington, and Canada. Ethnic synods on a national scale flourished, and parishes and seminaries reflected ethnic rather than confessional realities. Lutherans remained mostly introverted. Although there was some assimilation in life-style, the question remained unanswered as to how such assimilation expressed itself theologically or ethically.

Lutherans were nevertheless faced with several challenges. The new historical-critical method applied to biblical studies in Europe affected American Lutherans because it raised questions about the Bible. Was the Bible the inspired word of God, or was it a book containing ancient notions no longer valid, such as the conviction that the earth is flat? A second challenge was Darwin's theory of evolution: if there is a biological link between animals and humans, how does one distinguish between them in terms of salvation?

But the issue which caused the most controversy among Lutherans (many of whom had become yoked to the Reformed in many parishes, especially in the East) was the Calvinist-Reformed doctrine of election (or predestination). John Calvin had taught a doctrine of "double predestination," meaning that God has predestined some to salvation, and others to damnation. When questioned as to how, and by what signs, one could know whether one was to be saved or damned, Calvinists tended to respond that these signs are evident in the life-style of believers.

The Ohio and the Missouri synods debated the doctrine in the early 1880s, but came to no conclusion; most Lutherans supported the Lutheran Confessions' position that God elects believers in Christ and no one can know whom God condemns. Some Norwegian Lutherans linked the debate on election to the question of conversion: is it a human decision, God's decision, or both? They were equally unsuccessful in finding a resolution.

◇————————————————————————◇

Manifest Destiny and Lutheran Identity

There were almost ten million Lutherans in the United States by 1900. President Theodore Roosevelt referred to the Lutheran Church as being destined to become one of America's greatest churches; others called it a sleeping giant. But Lutherans were still too much divided to share these visions. Ethnic loyalty, confessionalism, apathy, and other negative forces still predominated. Most Lutheran congregations preferred to worship in a language other than English. Lutheranism before World War I was virtually a foreign-language church, identified by confessional

Luther Monument, Washington, D.C.

ties to Europe rather than by any obvious involvement in what has been called "the lively experiment" of religion in America.

Lutherans in the East found some common ground with regard to the authority of the Bible, the normative role of the Augsburg Confession, and liturgy. By 1918, Northeastern Lutherans had merged with the Southern Lutherans, and that part of Lutheranism looked more promising than any other, if one judged by signs of unity. But it was the common German heritage that made much of this possible; other Lutherans seemed more divided because of their diversity of inherited language—Danish, Swedish, Norwegian, and Finnish.

Nathan Söderblom, Bishop of Sweden

The year 1917, the four hundredth anniversary of Luther's reformation, did much to awaken a sleeping part of Lutheranism. World War I also changed the existing climate. Since almost everything German was met with hostility (German books and even some parochial schools were burned), Lutherans were forced to scramble to be identified as Americans opposed to imperial Germany. The Inner Mission Board of the General Synod, led by the Ministerium of Pennsylvania, negotiated with the Red Cross and the military services to find ways Lutherans could support the war effort. Various Lutheran church bodies met in 1917 to create a central Lutheran board for wartime service, resulting in the establishment of a "Commission for Soldiers' and Sailors' Welfare." The Commission, with offices in Washington, D.C., recruited chaplains, provided workers in hospitals, and maintained contact with all Lutherans serving in the military. Financial support for these activities doubled the established goals. Most Lutheran church bodies supported the Commission, with the exception of the Missouri Synod, which suspected the Commission of planning church mergers.

But Lutheran cooperation waned after the war. Post-war issues like Prohibition and pacifism did not concern them very much. Most supported Prohibition, since it echoed early immigrants' Pietism, which forbade drinking; very few supported pacifism.

Ethnic solidarity was cracking in favor of movement toward unity. Theological colloquies and inter-synodical meetings resulted in some progress in that direction. In 1918, the "National Lutheran Council" was created. It represented most synods (with the exception of the Missouri Synod) as well as the United Lutheran Church, which was a merger of several Eastern Lutheran groups. The United Lutheran Church's "Washington Declaration" of 1920 spoke of a "catholic spirit" and echoed the ecumenical direction of the Augsburg Confession. Lutherans joined the international Lutheran conference held in Eisenach, Germany, in 1923, and the second international conference even elected John A. Morehead, the American executive director of the National Lutheran Council, to be its head. The Iowa and the Joint Ohio Synods managed to merge in 1930 to form an "American Lutheran Church." They were joined by the small Buffalo Synod and a Texas synod related to the Iowa Synod. However, Lutheran unity was still a distant goal.

The ecumenical movement, pioneered in Europe by the Lutheran bishop Nathan Söderblom of Sweden who convened the first international meeting in 1925, had some effect on Lutherans in America. So did the international mission movement, which was linked to the quest for Christian unity around the world. After World War II, a "Lutheran Evangelism Council" initiated a national mission program with the slogan "preaching teaching reaching" (PTR), and campus ministries were started in colleges and universities.

New mergers of larger church bodies now occurred. A new "American Lutheran Church" united most Scandinavians in the Midwest in 1960; the Lutheran Church in America replaced the United Lutheran Church and included some smaller Lutheran groups in the East in 1962; and the Evangelical Lutheran Church in Canada was organized in 1968. All these new church bodies joined the Lutheran World Federation and began to exert some influence on world Lutheranism. Only the Missouri Synod stayed on the sidelines, insisting that confessional unity required theological conformity.

Lutherans in America from the beginning were so preoccupied with their own internal problems that they, perhaps unknowingly, ignored

the nation's dreams of a manifest destiny. They never linked their quest
for identity with it, and, in this sense, they injected a note of irony into
American denominationalism which, in its early Protestant/Puritan versions, shared end-time visions with political idealists.

Dreams of manifest destiny are only infrequently expressed today,
given the change in politics, science, and religion since World War II.
It may be more important for Lutherans in America to discover their
ecumenical role in the midst of a growing Christian and religious
pluralism than to worry about Americanization. They may have to face
the issue raised by Samuel S. Schmucker in the 1850s, which was whether
to be more exclusively Protestant (in the anti-Roman Catholic sense),
or to be pioneers in ecumenism in accordance with the Augsburg
Confession of 1530. Lutheranism could indeed become the giant of
American denominationalism, awake and ready to fulfill the destiny
dreamed of in early Lutheranism, namely to be a reform movement
within the church catholic both in the United States and abroad.

Missionary Connections

Forays by Church and State

Lutherans from the beginning had been engaged in missionary efforts among non-Christians, but encounters with non-Christians were quite limited in the sixteenth century. One sixteenth-century Lutheran, Primas Truber, worked as a reformer in Laibach (now Yugoslavia) and, when exiled by the Catholic authorities, found refuge in Tübingen, Germany. He translated the New Testament and parts of the Lutheran Confessions into Slovenian, and published works in Croatian. He even provided a catechism printed in Cyrillic letters for Turkish Muslims. But Lutheran missionary work in Yugoslavia was cut short by the "Counter Reformation," since the territory was ruled by Catholics.

It was not until the beginning of the eighteenth century, however, that Lutheran missionary efforts were undertaken in earnest by Halle Pietists in cooperation with Scandinavian governments. The Danish government and Halle Pietists collaborated in launching a Lutheran missionary program in Tranquebar, India, where the Danes had established a colony in 1624. Frederick IV, king of Denmark, now wanted to send missionaries to the native population to help his chaplains serving the Danish military and administrative personnel there. His court chaplains made contact with Halle, and recruited the Francke disciple Bar-

Graduating class of the Theological Seminary of the Leipzig Mission,
Tranquebar, India

tholomäus Ziegenbalg, who left for Tranquebar in 1706. Ziegenbalg
was well qualified for the mission, having learned Tamil, the native
language, as well as being ready to immerse himself in the culture there.
Ziegenbalg produced a Tamil grammar, and translated the New Testament, Luther's Catechisms, and a service book. Gifts from Germany
and Denmark helped him build a church which he dubbed "New
Jerusalem." King Frederick IV inaugurated an annual grant to the
church, and a Danish Mission college supported the Indian missionary
program after 1714. Disciples of Ziegenbalg, among them Christian F.
Schwartz, who served there for forty-eight years, continued his work
in New Jerusalem. When the Danish government sold its colony to
England in 1845, the Leipzig Missionary Society supported the Lutheran
pastors there; later, the Church of Sweden assumed part of the support.
The mission in Tranquebar eventually evolved into the Tamil Evangelical Lutheran Church.

The Lutheran mission in India provided a good model for future missions. The Pietist missionaries, though sponsored by various governments, tried very hard to avoid being the stereotypical colonialist missionaries who forced prospective converts to adopt their own cultural and political customs before accepting them as responsible Christians. The Moravians from Herrnhut were particularly adept at establishing very ecumenical missions in line with the Augsburg Confession. They were motivated by the missionary vision of Count Zinzendorf, their benefactor, who was convinced that Lutheranism is an effective means of linking biblical Christianity with all religions and cultures. Zinzendorf was friendly with the Danish government, and the Moravian missionaries Christian David and Hans Egede were soon sent to the Danish colony of Greenland; others were sent to the West Indies, India, Dutch Guyana, southern Africa, and North America.

German and Scandinavian Pietist missionaries also travelled to the arctic north. In 1716, the Norwegian missionary Thomas von Westen organized a mission among the Lapps, which was sponsored by the Danish court. Eventually, he founded several congregations and a small seminary there. The Swedish court followed suit in its northern territories.

All these early Lutheran missionary programs soon received support and training from various national and regional missionary societies. The Berlin Missionary Society, founded in 1824, was supported by the church at large, noble families who wanted to create "a faithful witness to the gospel in a faithless age," and by about eight hundred women's auxiliary societies. It sent missionaries to the various German colonies in South Africa (1834), east Africa (1891) and China (1898). The Barmen-Rhenisch Missionary Society, organized in 1819 by German Lutherans, sent missionaries to southwest Africa, Borneo, Sumatra, and New Guinea. The North German Bremen Society, combining Lutheran and Reformed missionary efforts after 1836, sent missionaries to New Zealand, India, and African colonies. The Leipzig Society, organized in 1838, took on much of the work done in India from 1845. The Gossner Society, headquartered near Berlin, sent missionaries to Australia but turned to India when no colony could be established in Australia. Other German missionary societies often duplicated the work others had done.

Each of the Scandinavian nations had its own missionary society doing work in Scandinavian colonies: the Danish Copenhagen Missionary college was established in 1714 and sent its missionaries to India; the Norwegian missionary society sent missionaries mainly to Madagascar; and the Swedes worked in east Africa, Finland and Lapland. The Finns organized a missionary society in 1859, giving special attention to Africa and the province of Hunan in China.

In North America, the various Lutheran church bodies organized missionary societies to support the work of their particular ethnic home churches.

The nineteenth century was truly the "century of mission," and Lutherans played their part. Anglicans and Methodists led the missionary efforts abroad, cooperating with Lutherans and other European church bodies. There was at first great optimism regarding the future of a Christian world, but European and North American missionaries exported Western culture and customs, as well as Christian disunity, which dampened the original optimism. It became clear that strong efforts were needed to unify missionary efforts and to encourage the "younger churches" to provide leadership from their own ranks. A World Mission Conference, held in Edinburgh in 1910, was addressed by seventeen Asian church leaders who pushed hard for ecumenical cooperation. It was clear that bringing Christ to the nations (Matt. 28:19) had, more often than not, resulted in nationalizing Christ.

◊ ———————————————————————————— ◊

Evangelism in the Third World

By the end of the nineteenth century, Lutherans had established churches on all the continents. The Tranquebar church exemplifies the history of Lutheran missions, revealing the struggle to maintain loyalty to the Lutheran Confessions while adapting Lutheranism to the surrounding culture. In Tranquebar, Lutherans accepted British rule when the British government bought the Danish colony in 1845. Politically, they favored the status quo. The most divisive issue, the Indian caste system, was treated with "pastoral prudence." The system was not criticized as long as congregations did not split over the issue or condone discrimination among their own members, for criticism would evoke a response from

Jerusalem Church, Tranquebar, India

the government. The Basel Mission and North American Lutheran churches helped support the Tranquebar mission. In 1874, the Church of Sweden guided the Tamil mission in its adoption of an episcopal polity.

German Lutherans eventually sponsored a mission in Calcutta, which resulted in the organization of the Gossner Evangelical Lutheran Church, named after Johannes E. Gossner, who was a Berlin pastor and had led the Calcutta mission. In 1975, the nearly four million Lutherans in India united in a federation of church bodies known as the United Evangelical Lutheran Churches in India. This federation maintains cordial relations with the other Christian groups in India— after all, Christians constitute less than three percent of the population of nearly eight hundred million.

How Lutherans fared in the Third World is most dramatically illustrated in the rise of the Protestant Christian Batak Church in Indonesia. Indonesia was a Dutch colony in Southeast Asia until it gained its independence as a republic in 1949. It consists of over three thousand islands—the largest being Sumatra and Kalimantan (formerly Borneo)—and has a population of one hundred sixty million.

The Rhenish Mission Society sent Lutheran missionaries there, and Missionary Ludwig I. Nommensen moved to Sumatra from Borneo in 1861 to convert the Batak people. Two American missionaries had preceded Nommensen to Sumatra, but the Bataks killed them in 1834, presumably because they did not know the Batak language. In 1848, the Dutch Bible Society sent a linguist there who studied local customs, translated part of the Bible, and produced a dictionary. Nommensen was able to use this material as a foundation for further study of Batak culture, in which he fully immersed himself. The Bataks had their own missionary society after 1899, and sent their missionaries to the other islands. By the time Nommensen died in 1918, he had created village churches and schools, and had facilitated economic improvement. He was always concerned with the preservation of the Batak heritage.

The theological basis of the Batak mission is the declared intention of the Rhenish Mission to be "non-confessional" and to exhibit "a fraternal union" between Lutherans and other Protestants, especially the Reformed. Although it acknowledged differences, the Rhenish Mission was convinced the confessional differences should not hinder cooperation for the cause of Christ. That is why the first constitution of the Batak Lutheran Church in 1881 does not mention the Lutheran Confessions, even though missionary work was heavily influenced by them and by Pietism. In 1930, Lutheran and other Protestant Bataks jointly confessed that the Bible is the only true source of their faith, having expression in trinitarian baptism.

Batak Lutherans sought to distance themselves from their Dutch and German roots during the dictatorship of Adolf Hitler in Germany. The conflict had begun to affect their homeland, since the Dutch authorities imprisoned German missionaries after 1940 on the grounds that they were part of the enemy that had invaded Holland. Having learned of the struggle among Lutherans in Germany which culminated in the 1934 Barman Declaration against tyranny, the Bataks proceeded to create their own confession and constitution, declaring themselves a Protestant body grateful to the Lutheran tradition.

A "Batak Confession" was drafted in 1951, based on the Augsburg Confession but incorporating the contemporary context of mission. Its preface clearly rejects the religious points of view expressed by Roman Catholics, radical Christian sects such as Pentecostal, heathen cults, and Islam. The Confession, in accordance with the dogma of the Trinity expressed in the creeds, declares that Scripture is sufficient as the Word of God, and affirms justification by faith and not works. It further declares that Sunday is a holy day, that heathen food regulations no longer apply to them, and that believers are assisted by angels. It acknowledges the validity of the Lutheran Confessions without referring to them explicitly, but asserts that the church must, in every age, make its own confession in the face of adversity and heresy.

The Lutheran Confessions have been translated into Indonesian languages, and a volume of *Key Words* of Lutheran theology was published in 1983. The Batak Church Constitution provides for a structure best fitted to the needs of a mission church: a presiding bishop called "ephorus" (an ancient Spartan title for an administrator); district "superintendents" (a legacy from the Germans); pastors of "resorts" (small clusters of congregations); and a teacher/preacher for each parish. The Batak church also ordains women, and these "Bible-women" do much of the evangelizing.

Indonesian Lutherans, numbering about three million, are very influential in Indonesia: Nommensen University has provided higher education for its young people since 1954; there is an ecumenical seminary in Jakarta, the capital; Lutherans serve in the government, and have participated in many areas of social and political reform.

A counterpart to the Lutheran mission in Indonesia are the Lutherans in Tanzania. Tanzania, formerly the African colonies of Tanganyika and Zanzibar, has been an independent republic since 1961. German missionaries, led by Bruno Gutmann, a missionary from Leipzig familiar with tribal languages and deeply committed to preserving African culture, began their mission work there in 1890. The Germans were forced to leave during World War I, and the British mission agencies replaced them. The British were joined by Scandinavian and North American Lutherans from the Augustana Synod in the 1920s and 1930s. Danish, Norwegian, and Finnish missionaries were sent to Tanzania when they could no longer work in China. After World War II, the Church of Sweden sent Bengt Sundkler, a university professor who became the bishop of the Tanzanian Lutheran Church.

A Federation of Lutheran Churches of Tanganyika was organized in 1958. Tanzanian Lutherans have always been proud of their African heritage, and have done their own missionary work from the beginning.

They have been led by skilled bishops, theologians, and church leaders like Josiah Kibira (1925–88) who served a term as president of the Lutheran World Federation.

Tanzanian Lutherans have always adhered to the Lutheran Confessions, specifically the Augsburg Confession and Luther's Small Catechism, as "explanations" of Holy Scripture. Pastors are trained in Confessional Lutheranism at Makumira Lutheran Theological College in Usa River, near Arusha. Synodical Bible schools train evangelists, deacons, and parish workers to continue the mission work at home and in neighboring countries. Some missionaries have served in Europe and North America. A Tanzanian missionary serving a parish in Anderstorp, Sweden, was told that he was the living gospel in their midst.

Missionary efforts in the Third World have reflected the two opposing strands of Pietism and orthodoxy in Lutheranism. An example of orthodoxy is the Evangelical Lutheran Church in Brazil, whose more than twenty thousand members reflect both the colonialist and the confessionalist aspects of mission. As the number of German immigrants increased, so did their disagreements. The Missouri Synod had begun sending missionaries to Brazil in 1900, and many of the conservative German immigrants were attracted to it. A seminary patterned after Concordia Seminary in St. Louis was established as early as 1903. This branch of Brazilian Lutheranism became a district within the Missouri Synod in 1904 and remained so until 1980. Its confessional stance, according to which *The Book of Concord* is held to be "the only correct exposition of Holy Scripture . . . and does not permit any alteration of this norm," for a long time inhibited friendly relations with other Lutheran Churches in Brazil. Efforts have been made since 1959 to conduct dialogues with the much larger and more liberal Evangelical Church of the Lutheran Confession in particular.

A Lutheran mission among German settlers in South Africa was begun in Cape Town in 1820. Little was done to combat apartheid until after World War II, when a majority of the South African churches integrated their membership and thus came into conflict with first the British rulers of the territory, and later the independent South African government that was established in 1961. At its meeting in Budapest in 1984, the Lutheran World Federation suspended two South African Lutheran church bodies because they refused to admit nonwhites as members. Black South African Lutherans had taken the confessional

Christ Church, Jerusalem

position that in times of adversity, certain adiaphora were no longer debatable but rather a matter of loyalty to the gospel; the system of apartheid persecuted blacks and had therefore become a gospel issue (*status confessionis*, as stated in *The Book of Concord*). Both churches agreed with this position, recanted, and were reinstated to the Lutheran World Federation at its assembly in Curitiba, Brazil, in 1990. In this case, Lutherans remained loyal to their confessional tradition.

Third World Lutherans represent about one-sixth of the sixty million Lutherans around the world. There are about 4.7 million Lutherans in Africa alone, most of them living south of the Sahara desert, with centers in Tanzania, Madagascar, Cameroon, Ethiopia, Liberia, and Nigeria. Lutherans in predominantly Catholic Latin America, including the Caribbean, number about 1.3 million.

German Lutheran missionaries came to Australia in 1838, some of them representing the orthodox views of the old Prussian union. August L. Graebner, a professor from Concordia Seminary in St. Louis, organized the New Zealand Lutherans in the 1890s. There are now about five million Lutherans in Australia and Australasia.

There is even a sprinkling of Lutherans in the Middle East, where German Lutherans and Anglicans established a joint diocese in Jerusalem in 1841, even though the two communions differed doctrinally on the interpretation of the Eucharist. The bishop, either Lutheran or Anglican, would ordain Lutheran pastors on the basis of the Augsburg Confession and Anglican pastors on the basis of the Thirty-Nine Articles.

Since 1970, Lutheran mission boards and societies have tried to avoid the charge of missionary efforts being tied to colonialist interests by designating their evangelism efforts in the Third World "church cooperation" rather than "mission." But the roots of Third World Lutheranism are still European and North American, and therefore the tension between faith and culture is still quite strong.

◇───────────────────────────────────────◇

Ways of Cooperation

Lutheran missions in the Third World experienced the pitfalls resulting from having their geographic roots in Europe and denominational ideology in North America. Some of these pitfalls included lack of communication between the various missions, often in the same region; apathy in the face of cultural aberrations such as racial segregation or the caste system; and the propagation of theological anachronisms in orthodoxist or Pietistic isolation. The European and North American churches simply extended their field of action without considering either a common strategy or the ecumenical thrust of the Lutheran Confessions. As a result, the Lutheran mission churches often re-fought old battles or became mired in the problems exported by the home churches. There were notable exceptions, to be sure, such as the Batak church in Indonesia. But, after a century of missionary effort, Lutheranism in the Third World still has a long way to go to overcome these pitfalls.

The situation has changed somewhat since World War II. Although the Lutheran churches in Africa, Asia, Australasia, and Latin America are eager to accept the assistance of outside churches, they have used the ecumenical movement to get better acquainted with each other, at least in their own region. The Lutheran World Federation has sponsored continental conferences, especially in Africa. Its Department of Studies undertook research projects such as a study of the church's identity and its service to the whole human being, and this study brought a number of African churches together in the 1970s.

African regional conferences were held to deal with evangelism, self-support, theological education, and ways to combat racism. Having experienced a sense of solidarity, some Lutheran leaders called for an

"African Confession." The "Lutheran Radio Voice of the Gospel" began broadcasting from Addis Ababa, Ethiopia in 1963. Its broadcasts reached beyond Africa to Asia and were in eighteen languages. It was silenced in 1977 when a new government assumed power. An All-Africa Lutheran Churches' Information Center and Coordination Center was established in Arusha, Tanzania in 1978. Consultations on theology in the African context were launched that same year, beginning with a consultation on Luther and Lutheranism in the context of the new cultural and political situations existing in Africa. In 1980, Lutherans helped form a Joint Christian Ministry in western Africa to reach the tribes living on the plains. Theological schools and seminaries there are now exchanging ideas on curricula in order to arrive at common strategies for ministry.

Lutherans in Asia, who are a tiny minority, joined other Protestant and Orthodox churches in 1973 to form the Christian Conference of Asia, which affirms the credal basis (the authority of Scripture and the ecumenical creeds) of the World Council of Churches. Designed to facilitate cooperation in the mission efforts of the fifteen national church councils and over one hundred churches it represents, the Conference has its administrative headquarters in Tokyo; its communication center is in Hong Kong; its brain-trust devising development, evangelism, and theology is in Bangkok; and its center for education is in Manila.

Asia Lutheran News, a Lutheran newspaper, was founded in 1977 and was expanded into the *Asia Lutheran Press Services* in 1986. An Asia Lutheran Church Leaders Conference was organized to assist cooperation between Lutherans. But, since Lutherans are so widely dispersed in Asia, it is vital for them to cooperate with others. The Asia Program for the Advancement of Training and Studies was organized with the participation of other Protestants. It sponsors workshops and symposia such as the symposium on Luther, held in 1983.

Similar developments toward regional cooperation have occurred in Latin America, beginning in 1951 with an all-Latin-American Lutheran conference in Curitiba, Brazil, and sponsored by the Lutheran World Federation. This conference was concerned primarily with refugees and the large number of unchurched German and Scandinavian immigrants. In 1956, a Lutheran seminary serving all Spanish-speaking churches on the continent was founded in Buenos Aires, and was merged with an older Protestant seminary to form the Evangelical Institute for Advanced

Studies in 1970. Major concerns of these cooperative efforts have been attracting ethnic groups who have shied away from integration into Latin American culture, and the problems of urbanization, unemployment, and poverty. As a result, the Latin American Lutheran Council, encompassing Lutherans from all the traditions including the Missouri Synod, was organized in 1965 to deal with these concerns.

Lutherans have, at times, even managed to cooperate intercontinentally. One example is the Third World Lutheran Theological Educators' Conference, held in 1988 in Sao Leopoldo, Brazil, which dealt with the topic "Rethinking Luther's Theology in the Contexts of the Third World." Educators from Africa, Asia, Latin America, and North America met to exchange their views on Luther and to highlight their own particular context. They issued a common declaration in which they called for a theological reconsideration of the relationship between personal and social sin, reflecting the problems of the Third World. They also advocated curricular revisions in Lutheran seminaries which would instill a greater awareness of socio-cultural problems ranging from the treatment of women to racism. Also, they committed themselves to creating a network among the theological institutions of the Third World that would share curricular ideas and build a better partnership.

All these efforts toward greater cooperation among and between Lutherans and other Christians have considerably changed the image of Third World Lutheranism as an extension of Western culture. Some Third World Lutheran churches have recaptured the spirit of Luther's Reformation through their efforts to make Christian unity more visible.

CHAPTER 6

◇————————————————————————◇

World Lutheranism

———————————— ◇ ————————————

Joining the Quest for Unity

Expansion into the Third World led European and North American Lutherans to view themselves as a worldwide movement which needed to transcend ethnic and territorial boundaries. Lutherans around the world had become a family of strangers, with little, if any, contact with Lutherans beyond their respective countries and geographical regions.

In Europe, growing awareness of the governmental pressure to make the church an obedient servant of the state led German Lutherans to convene a General Evangelical Lutheran Conference in Hannover in 1868, at which fifteen hundred delegates representing all the territorial churches committed themselves to preserving "the true teaching of the gospel" as expressed in the Lutheran Confessions. The Conference vowed to wage a battle against "unbelief, false and worldly Christianity, and unionism" (a reference to government attempts to merge Lutherans and Calvinists). Contacts were made with Scandinavian and American Lutherans, especially with the General Council of the Evangelical Lutheran Church in America. The churches in Sweden, Norway, and France sent representatives to the second Conference in 1870, held in Leipzig.

Later Conferences revealed how difficult it was to achieve Lutheran unity. Some delegates spoke of the Conference as a convention of individuals rather than churches; others, particularly Scandinavians, accused the Germans of being too defensive about Lutheran Confessions. Confessionalists found the 1908 Conference too liberal, and organized a "Lutheran League" *(Bund)* to preserve loyalty to the Lutheran Confessions. Americans lobbied for a worldwide convention to demonstrate global Lutheran unity, but this was considered unrealistic in view of the political conflicts that were leading to World War I.

In Europe, people grew increasingly estranged from the church. It was no longer fashionable to belong to a church when German and Scandinavian intellectuals were propagating a faith in natural sciences and a do-it-yourself philosophy, expressed in the statement "I am the master of my fate." It was asserted that the world could exist without God. Ragnar Askmark, the Swedish churchman, described the situation well when he stated that to be educated and a Christian was a contradiction. Not only was there apathy towards Christianity, but some, like the philosopher Friedrich Nietzsche, demonstrated downright hostility toward it, declaring God dead.

This "de-churching," or secularization of European society, forced Christians in general, and Lutherans in particular, to seek closer ties with each other. One of the most influential pioneers of the movement for Christian unity was the Swedish archbishop Nathan Söderblom (1866–1931), who had been raised in the Christian student movement. In the student movement, which advocated ecumenical dialogue and experiences in order to overcome parochialism, Söderblom had learned that Christian unity is a prerequisite to mission both at home and abroad. The first World Conference on Mission, held in Edinburgh in 1910, had shown him how necessary it was to develop a network among all the churches, especially among "younger churches" in the Third World.

Söderblom campaigned for a world conference on Christian unity after World War I, contending that the post-war world needed not only peace but worldwide cooperation among churches. Since many church leaders agreed with him, such a conference was held in Stockholm in 1925 in commemoration of the Council of Nicea in 325, which had established the dogma of the Trinity as the basis for unity. The conference was intended to deal with "practical Christianity" rather than with matters of dogma. A Conference on Faith and Order was held in Lausanne, Switzerland in 1927, where nearly four hundred delegates from more than one hundred churches (with the exception of the Roman

Catholic Church) agreed that God desires Christian unity, and that this unity ought to be pursued with deliberate speed. Eventually, a Conference on Life and Work constituted a second component of the ecumenical movement to work for international cooperation to improve life on earth. Söderblom spoke to the delegates at this conference, declaring that he had caught a glimpse of the united church, which was a still-distant goal that should never be abandoned.

American Lutherans had not given up their dream of demonstrating global Lutheran unity. The National Lutheran Council in the United States sent emissaries to Europe after 1918 to ascertain what kind of cooperation was possible among Lutherans. It was represented at the meeting of the General Evangelical Lutheran Conference in Leipzig in 1919, having established connections with the nearly one million Polish Lutherans of German origin. Joint decisions were made regarding relief work to the war victims.

American Lutherans were eager to foster cooperation with Third World Lutherans, and the National Lutheran Council created a committee in 1920 to develop a plan for a Lutheran world convention. The committee was led by Lauritz Larsen and Charles M. Jacobs. They suggested that a future international convention of Lutherans should deal with three topics: 1) the Lutheran Confessions; 2) methods and principles of church organization; and 3) the relation of Lutheran churches to the programs of Christian unity advocated by the growing ecumenical movement. The chairman of the National Lutheran Council, John A. Morehead, was chosen to work with the European churches to realize a plan to strengthen confessional Lutheranism throughout the world. After lengthy negotiations, it was agreed that the first Lutheran World Convention would be held in Eisenach in 1923, which was known for its connections to Luther and Johann Sebastian Bach.

One hundred fifty delegates, fifty registered observers, and hundreds of visitors gathered in Eisenach for that first Lutheran World Convention. The Convention was held in the shadow of an international economic crisis that would climax in the collapse of the U.S. stock market in 1929. The German Mark was already so inflated in 1923 that 4.2 million Marks equalled one dollar. There were other problems as well: German nationalism, which was to culminate in the National Socialism of Adolf Hitler, was growing; communism, exported from Russia after the 1917 Revolution, was also gaining popularity.

First Lutheran World Convention, Eisenach, Saxony, Germany (1923)

Söderblom was the strong speaker for Europe, urging for a unity that could transcend political and geographical boundaries. John Morehead spoke for the United States, advocating the establishment of a permanent platform to which Lutherans around the world could subscribe. Members of the Missouri Synod called for a "free conference" rather than a continuing Convention, for a free conference would not bind anyone to anything. Others strongly supported Morehead's proposal to give world Lutheranism an enduring voice. Theophilus Meyer spoke for Russian Lutherans (mostly German immigrants) who needed strong support in the face of atheistic communism.

The principal issue at Eisenach was Lutheran identity in the twentieth century. What did it mean to be a confessional Lutheran? A committee, composed for the most part of Germans, Scandinavians, and Americans, drafted five resolutions to deal with the issues. They were: 1) commitment to the Scripture as "the only source and infallible norm of all church doctrine and practice" and to the Lutheran Confessions, especially the unaltered Augsburg Confessions and Luther's Small Catechism, which were "pure expositions of the Word of God"; 2) international efforts to provide catechetical instruction for young people everywhere, using Luther's Small Catechism as the chief instrument for teaching; 3) continuation of post-war relief work "until the Lord shall put an end to distress"; 4) working for unification in conjunction with other Christian agencies, especially the Central Office for Protestant Relief, headquartered in Zurich; and 5) establishing an Executive Committee to continue the work of the Convention, its members being chosen according to a fair representation of participating countries and churches.

The future of a Lutheran international organization was thus assured. Lutherans had now joined the ranks of other bodies such as the Anglican Lambeth Conference (1876), the Calvinist Alliance of Reformed Churches Throughout the World Holding the Presbyterian System (1875), the Methodist Ecumenical Conference (1881), the Union of Old Catholic Churches (1889), the International Congregational Council (1891), and the Baptist World Congress (1905).

However, the Eisenach Convention was still unable to celebrate Lutheran unity in its worship service of thanksgiving, for unresolved differences prevented eucharistic fellowship. Nevertheless, the Convention had raised the issue of Lutheran identity as opposed to non-Lutheran Protestantism and Roman Catholicism. This issue was of particular importance to German, North American, and Third World Lutherans, because the problems they faced differed from those of Scandinavians. Scandinavian Lutherans were state churches, with very few other Christian churches on their territory. Lutherans in Germany had to contend with governments that tried to merge them with the Reformed. In the United States, Lutherans faced a growing religious pluralism safeguarded by laws separating church and state. Third World Lutherans were a small minority and confronted non-Christian religions.

The second Lutheran World Convention, held in Copenhagen in 1929, had more than one hundred delegates representing the various experiences of Lutherans in the world. There was more discussion of Lutheran identity, with particular attention paid to Luther's Small Catechism as the most evangelical and ecumenical expression of the sixteenth-century Reformation. Ways of preserving Lutheran unity were discussed, and the Convention closed with a firm commitment to remain the universal voice of Lutheranism.

◇ ——————————————————————————————————— ◇

Encounter with Tyranny

When the German monarchy became a republic in 1918, Lutherans there faced a new situation. Territorial rulers had had veto power over the church, at first as "emergency bishops" *(Notbischöfe)* and then "supreme bishops" *(summi episcopoi)*, ever since the peace of Augsburg in 1555. Now the long emergency was over. Germany was now governed by representatives of various political parties. Twenty-eight churches formed a "League of Churches" *(Kirchenbund)* to negotiate a mutually satisfactory relationship between church and state. The state granted religious freedom to the Lutheran and Reformed churches, and an executive committee of the churches was formed to guard this freedom and negotiate other changes when necessary. The territorial churches gathered on a "day of churches" *(Kirchentag)* every three years to discuss various issues in the light of Scripture and the confessional traditions.

When the president of Germany, Paul von Hindenburg, officially transferred his office to Adolf Hitler in 1933, German Lutherans were confronted with a government hostile to their Judeo-Christian tradition. The National-Socialists (Nazis) promised to create a new and powerful Germany. They had gained their power as a result of the rise of nationalism after Germany's defeat in World War I and the dire economic conditions. Interest in religion declined in the wake of the ongoing secularization of the new political situation. Adopting a racist stance grounded in the old myths of a Nordic super-race called "Aryan," the new German government coordinated all sectors of public life to engage in a struggle against communism and Judaism, its perceived enemies. Communists were viewed as the Slavic menace that threatened racial purity and Western culture; Jews were blamed for Europe's economic woes and seen as greedy sub-human "Semites."

The Nazi government declared its support of "a positive Christianity," which referred to churches that "did not violate the morality of the German race." Nazi Lutherans, known as "German Christians" *(deutsche Christen)* had gained one-third of the seats in the Prussian parliament as early as 1932. Hitler appointed Ludwig Müller, a Prussian Nazi pastor, to be a "bishop of the realm" *(Reichsbishof)*, a move

Adolf Hitler at the Reich Party Conference with Catholic Abbot Alban Schachtleiter, Reich Bishop Müller, and German Christian Reichsleiter Christian Kinder (shaking hands)

supported by a majority of the delegates to the Wittenberg Assembly of the National Synod, now organized into ten territorial segments.

The "platform of the German Christians" applauded Hitler for reviving "the German spirit of Luther" and "heroic piety"; agreed with the policy against "racial mixing," especially concerning relations with Jews; repudiated any ecumenical relations between churches; and asserted that the only valid factor was "faith in the national mission" given to Germans by God. Thus "the powers of Reformation faith" would lead "to the finest of the German nation."

Under the pressure applied by the German Christians, an opposition "emergency league" *(Notbund)* was organized under the leadership of Martin Niemöller, a submarine commander and hero of World War I. Nineteen territorial churches (Lutheran, Reformed, and United) sent one hundred forty delegates to Barmen in 1934, where they established a "Confessing Church" *(bekennende Kirche)*. The delegates signed a confession, the "Barmen Declaration," which affirmed six articles opposing the position taken by the German Christians. They were: 1) the gospel of Jesus Christ as revealed in Scripture, the creeds and the confessions are "the impregnable foundation" of the German Evangelical Church; 2) Jesus Christ is the only Lord of the church; 3) Jesus Christ works in the church through word and sacraments; 4) there are

Bishop Müller, on the steps of the Rathaus, Wittenberg, Germany,
with Nazi party officials

no special leaders other than Christ; 5) the state has no absolute power over the church; and 6) the church must remain free for its mission in the world. The new measures of the government were repudiated as "false teachings." When a second "Confessing Church" synod met in Dahlem and called for new emergency laws for the church to counteract those set by the German Christians, the Nazi government declared all actions of the Confessing Lutherans illegal.

By 1936, Lutherans in Germany were split into two factions, with the majority supporting the government. An overwhelming number of pastors signed the required oath of allegiance "to be obedient to the *Führer* of the German people and the state, Adolf Hitler . . . as befits an Evangelical German . . ." Those who did not sign were forbidden to exercise their public ministry and were no longer paid a salary. A number of bishops resigned in protest, and many pastors were jailed or drafted into the armed services. A few joined the existing underground resistance movement. Martin Niemöller was arrested in 1938,

Martin Niemöller   Dietrich Bonhoeffer

but Hitler gave orders not to kill him, and he survived the Hitler regime. Dietrich Bonhoeffer, a pastor and theologian, actively participated in a military plot to assassinate Hitler. The plot failed, and Bonhoeffer and others were executed in 1945, shortly before the end of the war.

In 1945, the surviving leaders of the "Confessing Church" met to establish the new Council of the Evangelical Church in Germany, and issued "The Stuttgart Declaration" confessing the inadequacy of their witness during the reign of Hitler. It confesses: "We have in fact fought for long years in the name of Jesus Christ against the spirit which found its terrible expression in National-Socialist government by force, but we accuse ourselves that we did not witness more courageously, pray more faithfully, believe more joyously, love more ardently. Now a new beginning is to be made in our churches."

In Norway, Lutheran resistance against Hitler, though under different conditions, was more effective than in Germany. When the Germans occupied Norway in 1940, a puppet government was set up to keep Norway in check, but this was opposed by a large majority of Norwegians, led by lawyers and pastors. Both sides based their argument on Luther. The new Nazi Department of Church and Education warned Lutheran clergy against resigning on the grounds that Luther had taught obedience to every government, because government was God-given. Bishop Eivind Berggrav, on the other hand, declared that what was at issue was an ancient Norwegian law dating from 1140 which stated that "the source of our laws" is reverence for Christ. He added that the new military government was placing itself above the law by demanding absolute obedience to the state—a position Luther never held.

Berggrav publicly identified Hitler as an embodiment of Niccolò Machiavelli's tyrannical "Prince" (*Führer* in his translation). In a lecture in 1941, Berggrav declared, "Tyranny's authority is like that of a crazy driver of a runaway horse," implying that such a driver or horse might have to be destroyed in order to maintain the safety of the streets. He concluded that those who remain silent share the guilt of disobeying Christ, for no government has the right to demand the souls of its citizens.

Berggrav remained under house arrest from 1942 to 1945. When the government began seizing Jewish property, the church protested, declaring that all the people had the same rights "according to the word of God," and that tyrannical governments need not be obeyed. The puppet government was faced with the choice of either enforcing its law, which would result in a bloodbath in Norway, or leaving the church alone. It chose to leave the church alone, especially since all the bishops had resigned, as had the vast majority of the pastors, who were supported by their congregations (only sixty of the thousand pastors remained in office under the puppet government). The church renounced its allegiance to the state in 1942 and became a self-governing folk church until 1945.

By 1989, East German Lutherans had learned the lessons of history. When an opportunity arose to throw off the shackles of tyranny, Lutheran churches became the staging areas for nonviolent protests. Lutheran church leaders were the avantgarde of what has been called the "quiet revolution of 1989," which resulted in the reunification of Germany.

◇ ———————————————————————————————————— ◇

The Lutheran World Federation

The work of the Lutheran World Convention virtually came to a halt during Hitler's reign (1933–1945). Its "American Section" tried to maintain contact with European Lutherans, but the outbreak of the war in 1939 severed all formal relations. The American Section of the Convention, in concert with the American National Lutheran Council, became the caretaker of the "orphaned mission" in the Third World, since German and Scandinavian mission societies were largely incapacitated. Under the leadership of Paul Empie, it organized "Lutheran World Action," initiating programs for the care of refugees and prisoners of war, and became the most effective arm of the Lutheran World Convention.

Post-war relief programs were initiated in 1945, and a huge Lutheran effort was undertaken to relieve post-war problems in many parts of the world. A fact-finding tour of Europe in conjunction with the Missouri Synod found ways to strengthen the already existing relief programs and helped European Lutherans survive the grim days after the war. Two meetings, one in Sigtuna, Sweden, and the other in Geneva, laid the foundation for a rebirth of the Lutheran World Convention.

In 1947, The Lutheran World Convention, assembled in Lund, Sweden, changed its name to the "Lutheran World Federation." The Swedish bishop Anders Nygren was elected the first president of the Federation, and the American Sylvester C. Michelfelder the first General Secretary. One hundred eighty-four delegates from forty-nine churches in twenty-two countries unanimously accepted a constitution intended to guide the proceedings. According to its constitution, world Lutherans are to be united as "a free association of Lutheran churches," for which the Federation can make no laws, and with which it cannot interfere from the outside. But the Federation will serve these churches in matters they themselves assign to it. The purpose of the Federation is

> ... to witness to the gospel of Jesus Christ as the power of God unto salvation; to nurture unity of faith and witness among the Lutheran churches in the world; to cultivate community and common studies; to further participation in ecumenical movements; to develop a unified Lu-

Signing the charter of the Lutheran World Federation at the first assembly in Lund, Sweden; seated are A. R. Wentz, Hanns Lilje, and J. P. Vanheest (signing)

theran initiative in mission and catechetics; and to help and support Lutheran groups in need of help.

Its constitution is grounded in two affirmations:

> acknowledgment of Holy Scripture as the only source and infallible norm of all teachings and practice in the church; and to view the Lutheran Confessions, especially the unaltered Augsburg Confession and Luther's Small Catechism, as true interpretation of Holy Scripture.

The Federation was to meet every five years, with interim business to be conducted by the president, general secretary, and an executive committee of twenty members. The Lutheran World Federation would be headquartered in Geneva, along with Federation commissions on theology, mission, and world service, with national committees established in the various member nations.

Subsequent assemblies highlighted the constitutional problem of whether or not the Federation could speak with authority for its member churches. What does being "a free association" mean? The Federation had already, in its first year of operations, pushed for a unified effort on the part of the Lutheran churches in missionary situations such as in Tanzania. The Christian Batak Church became a member of the Federation in 1952, yet this church makes no reference to the Lutheran Confessions despite a strong Lutheran presence. Since 1960, the Federation has urged stronger ties with other churches, especially the Roman Catholic Church, basing its arguments on the historical insight that the sixteenth century Lutheran Reformation was a reform movement within the Roman Catholic Church. Sometimes the ecclesiological problem in the Federation is debated in its publications, *The Lutheran World* and the *Lutherische Rundschau*.

The 1963 assembly, which met in Helsinki, acknowledged that not all Lutheran churches in the world share pulpit and altar fellowship and that Holy Communion had become an issue during assemblies. It tried to reinterpret the doctrine of justification, but was unsuccessful because members could not agree on the contemporary meaning of justification by faith. This assembly also called for the establishment of a research institute to realize the Lutheran mandate to be ecumenical. As a result, the Ecumenical Institute was founded in Strasbourg, France in 1965. The Institute's director and researchers set up ecumenical dialogues and pursue research projects in the context of Christian and human unity.

The 1984 assembly, meeting in Budapest, Hungary, claimed that altar and pulpit fellowship among member churches does exist and that a lack of such fellowship requires disciplinary action, such as exclusion from membership in the Federation.

The Federation succeeded in making a significant constitutional change at its eighth assembly in Curitiba, Brazil, in 1990. It changed the term *free association* to *communion*, thus giving it more of an ecclesial character than it previously had before. Issues of human rights and social justice have appeared on the agenda of the assemblies in increasing numbers, due to the socio-political problems in the Third World. Doctrinal and ethical concerns have thus merged, and have forced the Federation to expand its horizon.

Not all Lutheran churches belong to the Lutheran World Federation. The Lutheran Church–Missouri Synod is a notable holdout, since it espouses more doctrinal uniformity than the Federation is able to provide. Thus the question of Lutheran unity is still a thorny one: Will sixty million Lutherans around the world with around four hundred churches and organizations in more than one hundred countries ever be able to speak with one voice?

CHALLENGE

Proper God-talk

---◇---

A Christ-centered Mind

Human beings have practiced "God-talk" or "theology" (from the Greek *theologia*) since the beginning of time. They have always been preoccupied with the origin and destiny of whatever exists at the time. Religions refer to "god" as the source of all being, something absolute, the place or person responsible for what is ("the buck stops here"). Philosophers talk about "god" as an entity "beyond nature" (from the Latin *super naturam*), or "behind nature" (from the Greek *meta physis*). Most religions try, with dedicated sophistication, to keep God in the realm of timeless immorality.

The Bible's "God-talk" is different, for it attests to a god present in both space and time. The Bible's way of talking about god is neither supernatural nor metaphysical. The god of the Bible involves himself with people in specific places at specific times. He adopts the people of Israel ("I will take you as my people, and I will be your God," Exod. 6:7); he appears as a warlord defeating the Egyptians (Exod. 15:3); and he uses Assyrians to teach Israel a lesson about faithful relationships (Isa. 10:5, 30:15). The god of the Bible liberated the people of Israel from captivity, granting them freedom in a "holy land," and promised a future beyond death, "new heavens and a new earth" (Isa. 65:17).

97

According to the New Testament, God's promised new heaven and new earth was made possible by Jesus, who by his death on the cross atoned for all the wrongs done by all the people on earth. "God chose what is low and despised in the world ... so that no one might boast in the presence of God" (1 Cor. 1:28-29). The Christian apostle Paul called talk about the crucified and resurrected Jesus "a stumbling block to Jews and foolishness to Gentiles" (1 Cor. 1:23), for Jews still await the savior who will usher in the new heaven and the new earth, and Greeks reject all notions of a God dying on a cross.

Jesus, the incarnate Word who comes in the "fullness of time" (John 1:14-18, Gal. 4:4), embodies a faithful relationship. The first Christians defined this relationship as unconditional trust in Jesus rather than any reliance on human efforts to please or appease divine majesty. As the apostle Paul put it, "It is no longer I who live, but it is Christ who lives in me.... I live by faith in the Son of God, who loved me and gave himself for me" (Gal. 2:20).

Many Christians, however, forgot the radical declarations of Peter, Paul, and John that one's right relation with God is grounded in one's total faith in what Jesus did, not in what one does without Jesus. Employing pre-Christian Greek and Roman philosophy, theologians developed a system one could call "middle class spirituality," which focused on the cooperation between divine grace and a human being's efforts. The key features of this system adopted by the church, which are based on the assumption that a personal decision activates faith in God and that this faith is kept alive by one's own efforts, were—and still are—the ingredients of many sermons and Sunday School lessons. They sound like this:

> You are a creature of God, but have been born with a tendency to violate God's divine mandate to do good. You still have the ability to do some good, so be a good Samaritan and help create more justice in the world. None of your deeds will be sufficient to save you from punishment for the original sin you have inherited from Adam and Eve. But your good works will erect a moral platform on which you can stand with a sense of pride; offer these moral deeds to God on Sunday mornings in church, where you will receive divine grace to add to them. God's Word and Sacrament will give you a sense of fulfillment along your journey from this life to the next.

Exhortations like these assume a difference among believers. Some may reach a high level of faith and therefore receive special recognition in the church, which rewards high achievers with special positions and honors, regarding them as "saints." The enticement of honors has always been a part of the spice of life, especially religious life. Luther called it a "do-it-yourself" faith propagated by "pig theologians" who enjoy bathing in the mud produced by intellect and pride. These theologians tell people to rely on their own individual efforts to please God, and then provide a rationale for the church (which they declare to be the mediator between God's grace and individual good works) to offer forgiveness for sins.

When life becomes meaningless, however, and when one is drowning in despair, this kind of do-it-yourself faith does not work, and this kind of pastoral care is most unpastoral. When the bottom has dropped out, one discovers that one's own ego power is reduced to zero and that it takes two to believe, for one must borrow faith from someone still strong in faith when one's own faith is gone. When one is in doubt and despairs over the meaning of life, when one is close to denying the very existence of God, it is a word from outside that promises radical change and brings comfort. The biblical God is a lover who offers "good news" in the crucified Christ, who endows victims of ego power with gospel power.

In the sixteenth century, Luther rediscovered this God of the Bible and the Bible's way of talking about Jesus. He called such talk a "theology of the cross" because its focus is on Jesus "the crucified God." "Learn Christ and Him crucified," he told a friend searching for proper God-talk. "To seek God outside Jesus is the devil." All theology—all God-talk—must be Christ-minded, according to Luther, meaning that the cross of Jesus is the only true source of knowledge about God we have. Anything else is sheer speculation. No mystical contemplation or logical deduction can lead one to find God in one's inner self. Speculating on nature does not lead to knowledge of God's super-nature. To speculate about God without Jesus, either in nature or in time, merely projects one's own image. "What is above us is none of our business," Luther told Erasmus of Rotterdam when Erasmus was speculating about whom God might love or not love, and about other aspects of God's divinity. To Luther, such speculations were examples of false worship created by speculative reasoning, which the Bible calls "idolatry." This kind of reasoning tames and domesticates God, and "put[s] him into a purse, or shut[s] him up in a chest" (*BC* 366:13). Luther declared that to play god by using one's human reason to search for God is to commit the "original sin" depicted in the story of the serpent wooing Adam and Eve by tempting them to "be like God" (Gen. 3:5). He labeled this speculative talk about God without Jesus a "theology of glory" that tries to preserve the glory of God as an invisible, majestic entity uninvolved with our human quest for salvation.

But for Luther God-talk is precisely talk about salvation—about a God who loves humanity and woos people back to himself. The Bible's God descends to the world and joins people in space and time, between birth and death. God the "father" of Jesus enters the world as a baby born of a refugee named Mary, lives an ordinary life in Israel as the man Jesus of Nazareth, and dies on a cross erected by the Roman army. This kind of God-talk is truly an offense to those who cling to traditional religiosity, which professes faith in a deity aloof from the world. Traditional religiosity affirms a God to whom one must ascend by way of moral achievements, mystical contemplation, and rational speculation. But Luther insisted, "Our theology is certain, because it snatches us away from ourselves and places us outside of ourselves, so that we do not depend on our own strength, conscience, person or works, but rather depend on that which is outside ourselves, that is, on the promise and truth of God who cannot deceive." Such talk was a comfort to people who had vainly tried to ascend to God, having been convinced that they were created to please God through their own efforts.

To Luther and his reform movement, theology is not just an academic tool to explain the Christian faith or develop dogmas to control the faithful. Instead, God-talk focuses on Christ, God's self-revelation; it is the only rule in the grammar of faith and Christian living, the function of which is to keep one's focus on Christ alone. Like a snowplow, theology clears the road so that one's future with God can be discerned plainly. Proper God-talk does not explain or "prove" the existence of God. It challenges human pride, lays bare the ego, and opens the way to a childlike faith in what God in Christ does for us. In this sense, proper God-talk is the means by which Christians live the praise and thanksgiving for what God has done in Christ. Christ-centered God-talk leads to true worship, to adoration of the God who came to us in a manger and died for us on a cross, signs of His never-ending love.

◇───────────────────────────────────◇

Mandate and Promise

It took the early church three hundred years of reflection and sharp debate to arrive at the dogma of the Trinity, a doxological affirmation of God's revelation which is a part of worship rather than a theological explanation. The God of the Bible is simultaneously Creator and "Father" of Jesus, Redeemer and "Son," and Sustainer of the church as "Holy Spirit." This trinitarian language preserves the mystery of the one God known through his created order, his redeeming love, and spiritual power he bestows on the community of the faithful.

Although Lutheran theology focuses on the God who, in Christ, loves the ungodly (Rom. 4:5), it is aware of the hidden God who is not revealed. Luther learned about this biblical God from the apostle Paul and from St. Augustine (354–430). Even on the cross God was masked in the person of Jesus of Nazareth and therefore not fully revealed, although there are clear signs of his presence. According to the biblical understanding of history as God's time—salvation history—humanity sinned against God's most important commandment, "I am ... your God ... You shall have no other gods" (Exod. 20:2-3). Idolatry was rampant and laws to prevent chaos were needed. Israel's God in the Old Testament was known through his law and through the prophets who exhorted the people to remain faithful to the covenant God had made with them. As a result, Lutheran theology affirms the God-given mandate to preserve law and order.

Luther viewed the law in political and pedagogical terms: God instituted government, "temporal authority," to keep order in his creation. "Let every person be subject to the governing authorities" (Rom. 13:1). But governments, like all other human institutions, can become "beasts" creating idolatrous tyrannies (Rev. 13:1-4). Therefore God sends messengers and prophets to remind his creatures to remain faithful and to obey the basic law of faithfulness which is the first of the Ten Commandments.

The political function of the law is to preserve order by maintaining loyalty to God the Creator, but the pedagogical function of the law is to disclose sin (Rom. 3:20). In this sense, the law is a "disciplinarian" (from the Greek *paidagogos*, meaning "pedagogue") until Christ comes, "that we might be justified by faith" and not by law (Gal. 3:24). Luther describes this pedagogical function of the law as creating "inner struggle" or "temptation" (*Anfechtung* in German). In other words, creating internal anxiety is the way by which God alerts people to distrust laws as means to salvation and people should instead rely on the promise that salvation comes through faith in Christ alone. Thus the law drives people to the gospel in the same way that a plow prepares the ground to receive the seed.

The law shows the world as it really is: infested with sin, diabolically confused (from Greek *diaballein*, meaning "to be thrown about"), and sick unto death. Thus the law is like a mirror reflecting reality in the face of humanity's hopeless attempts to create the illusion that life is better than it really is.

Luther's move to view inner anxiety as the result of being unable to obey the divine mandate was quite a bold one, since there is just a hair's difference between pastoral comfort and self-destructive despair. After all, it was as a monk that Luther experienced his *Anfechtung*— not as an agnostic. Not all anxiety-ridden people make the transition from law to gospel, from recognizing their inability to obey the law to believing God's promises made through Christ. This is the specifically Lutheran contribution to theology. It recognizes the reality of sin, disclosed in one's inability to live according to God's law, and at the same time it proclaims God's solidarity with sinners. Thus the Lutheran Christ-centered mind points to the unity of the revealed and hidden God who is both victim and victor in the struggle against sin, evil, and death. The God of the Bible is revealed as victim on the cross on Good Friday, and as victor on Easter. As John the Baptist put it, Jesus is "the lamb of God who takes away the sin of the world" (John 1:29).

Lutheran theology therefore insists on proclaiming both law *and* gospel, the two aspects of the one Word of God. But it also insists that the focus of the proclamation must be on the gospel—on the divine promise, embodied in Jesus, of a new future beyond sin, evil, and death, and of a never-ending relationship with God. The ministry of Jesus has been summed up by his disciples, who quote him as saying, "The time is fulfilled, and the kingdom of God has come near; repent, and believe in the good news" (Mark 1:15).

The gospel promises are Christ-centered. In their most distilled form they simply assert that the resurrection of Jesus is the first step toward the new age to come, which is the "kingdom of God" linked to the lordship of Christ. The purpose of a Christian's life, then, is to make the transition to another world containing no sin, evil, or death, which had its birth at Easter and is symbolized by an empty tomb. Faith that is aware of this new world. "Faith is the assurance of things hoped for, the conviction of things not seen" (Heb. 11:1). Far from being utopian and idealistic, faith knows what is to come and shows the way to the well-known destination. That is why the first Christians were called people of "the Way," pilgrims to the promised land, who now "see in a mirror, dimly," but then will "see face to face" (1 Cor. 13:12). The first Christians were sure the end of the world was imminent. They gathered in communities and did no long-range planning, instead waiting with firm hope and praying, "Come, Lord Jesus" (Rev. 22:20).

Almost two millennia of Christian traditions have made the essentially simple story of Jesus' resurrection and promise of a new age much more complex, shaped by culture and ever-changing historical contexts. The time between the first coming of Jesus and his promised return has been a long and often mean time, filled with despair rather than hope, with apathy rather than passion, with doubt rather than faith.

Luther was convinced that his own time was the end-time, since it was plagued by a deformed church, yet pregnant with imminent new life. But he had merely revived the decisive element of Christian life: the awareness of the end, the "eschatological" existence (from the Greek *eschaton*, meaning "the last") which senses that last things come first.

Living in this mean time between Christ's first and second coming, waiting for the new age, is difficult. It may be compared to waiting in a physician's office to hear one's medical destiny. One waits patiently at first, but after a while one tries to relieve the anxiety by turning to magazines, reading what one would never otherwise want to read, or playing games one would really not otherwise play. One's mind collects all kinds of unnecessary items just because waiting has become boring, and going on waiting might even become dangerous.

Many Christian traditions compete with each other in the waiting room of history. Much has been accumulated to bring comfort to people in their anxiety, but these traditions need to be distilled, refined, and reformed through Christ-centered minds aware of the difference be-tween laws and promises, between the law and the gospel, between the old age and the new age to come. Proper God-talk will always attempt to view the world through the eyes of faith and will discern these differences, thus keeping the divine promise untainted.

◇—————————————————————————————————◇

Justified Freedom

Luther declared that the Christ-centered life is the only justified life. The "first and chief article" of faith is that one is made right before God by having faith in Jesus Christ who "was handed over to death for our trespasses and was raised for our justification" (Rom. 4:25). Luther insisted that this article of faith must not be compromised even when friend as well as foe want to make it less radical (*BC* 292:1, 5). One is "made right" with God (*dikaiosomai* in Greek), or "justified," by having complete trust in what God did in Christ—by "faith apart from works prescribed by the law" (Rom. 3:28). This faith is generated in the communication of what God did in Christ. "So faith comes from what is heard, and what is heard comes through the Word of Christ" (Rom. 10:17).

If one has the right relationship with God by faith, what is the purpose of doing anything besides believing? If faith is the "good work" of giving thanks for God in Christ, why do other good works? The Bible provides a clear though surprising answer: good works are not done to appease God's wrath towards sinners, they are done to serve the neighbor in need. A Christ-centered person loves the neighbor as well as him or herself. "You shall love the Lord, your God, with all your heart, and with all your soul, and with all your mind. . . . You shall love your neighbor as yourself" (Matt. 22:37, 39). Loving someone else as one loves oneself is the basic form of justice, for it brings the self and others into proper balance. It is the balance of freedom, for focusing on someone else liberates one from egotism. As Luther put it in his famous treatise, *The Freedom of the Christian*, "Christians live not in themselves but in Christ and their neighbor—in Christ by faith and in the neighbor by love. Faith liberates from self-righteousness by being caught up in God; and love binds one to the neighbor, just as God, in Christ, descends to sinners by love."

The cross is a splendid symbol of faith active in love. Its vertical bar signifies God's descent to save the ungodly through the Word, expressed in Jesus and his victory over death, thus wooing anxious hearts and minds to turn to faith. Faith is the Holy Spirit's gift that operates as the power of Christ between his first and second coming. Once filled with this faith, believers no longer need worry about how to please God or how to appease him with their own efforts, and instead are free to turn sideways, along the cross' horizontal bar, to extend their love to the world. The cross of Christ reminds Christ's disciples to move sideways into the world to proclaim the news of God's descent in the man Jesus. Once the Holy Spirit's gift of faith in the good news of God's act in Christ is received, believers are truly free to serve the world, God's old creation. The gift that comes with this faith is freedom, especially of the mind.

Moving horizontally like this may challenge conceptions popular among Christians, such as worship of success (as measured by worldly goods and a value system based on feeling good), on self-gratification, and on trust in human achievement to secure a better future. It is difficult to liberate one's mind from the lure of ego. "What's in it for me?" is the usual motive in any human action, be it voluntary or necessary. If one believes in God, one is tempted to do good in order to earn points with God. Since reward is a way of human life, why should it not be so with God?

The Lutheran theology of the cross, however, declares that one is right with God ("justified") when one lives solely by faith in Christ. That makes one truly free for what needs to be done in the world, since one no longer has to worry whether one will be rewarded or whether one will be accepted by the world. All good works done by faith are good in the sight of God. How liberating it is for a mind to be freed from moral anxiety! God may or may not reward what we have done—that is God's business, not ours. Thus freedom from self is a direct result of bondage to God. Luther called it being free by faith and slave by love. Like the cross, it is a balance between the divine gift of faith and love for the neighbor. Yet love is just the beginning; love extends to create justice and sometimes to ease suffering. The theology of the cross thus becomes an "ethics of the cross," wherein true freedom must face death in order to live truly.

A distinctive feature of Lutheranism is its view of human reason as an instrument of liberation. It allows a truly uninhibited Christian life-style, which, above all, is free to concentrate on the neighbor in need. No Christian will ever lack the occasion to exercise love and justice, for there will always be neighbors in need. But reason is needed to determine what should be done. Reason is therefore the tool to discern what is faithful in the sight of God and of the neighbor, to read the signs of the times, and then to undertake action for the sake of love and justice. Propelled by the vision of faith, reason is truly liberated to create a new morality and to direct it as a faithful witness to what God has done in Christ. Lutheran ethics start to function when one no longer asks "What's in it for me?"

For Lutherans, proper God-talk is biblical God-talk. It is a doxo-logical appreciation for the care that God—"Father, Son, and Holy Spirit"—takes of his creatures. At the bottom of Luther's Christ-centered theology is the trinitarian mystery of the hidden and revealed God. God reveals his divine identity in Christ and offers a foretaste of life beyond death, calling us to faithful witness during the period between Christ's first and second coming. Christ-centered God-talk opens up a window to the world as it is seen by God, a world in which his creatures have been promised eternal life, thus liberating them from the chains of ego. "So if the Son makes you free, you will be free indeed" (John 8:36).

Life in the Meantime

◇

Two Realms

Christians view history as the arena of God's activity. Luther likened God's involvement in history to the carnival season, climaxing on Shrove Tuesday, when people wear masks and indulge in a final fling of pleasure before the penitential Lenten season. But, promptly at midnight, Shrove Tuesday turns into Ash Wednesday. Then the masks come off, and believers gather at churches where they receive a cross of ashes on their foreheads as a reminder of the Last Day, when the world will end and final judgment will be rendered. Luther called human history the "mask" of God.

All events point to Jesus Christ, who is the mediator between the old and new ages. Ash Wednesday, the day of repentance, may come at any time, for "the day of the Lord will come like a thief in the night" (1 Thess. 5:2). Paul told the people of Athens, "[God] commands all people everywhere to repent, because he has fixed a day on which he will have the world judged in righteousness by a man whom he has appointed, and of this he has given assurance to all by raising him from the dead" (Acts 17:30-31). The time between Christ's first and second coming is a time for serious reflection and anticipation, and should evoke a change of mind, or "repentance" (from the Greek *metanoia*, meaning "change of mind"). That is why one must be alert to discern and interpret the signs of God's activity in one's own time.

There are two realms, both ruled by God. One is the realm of sin, death, and evil, which is the realm of God's "left hand," and is the law which preserves order so that fallen creation can survive until the new age. The other is the realm of faith, hope, and love, which is the realm of God's "right hand" and is the promise of a life beyond death in a new creation. The two realms, with their different realities, are like two circles that intersect to form the place and time between the departure and return of the resurrected Jesus. Christians live in this intersection. Thus Christian existence is two-faced: when facing oneself and other human beings, life is ruled by "Murphy's law," meaning something will always go wrong, and may become a disaster; when facing God with faith in Christ, everything seems right and salutary, and heaven seems guaranteed. Luther called it being "simultaneously righteous and a sinner" *(simul iustus et peccator)*. Everyone who has heard God's word as law and gospel, as mandate and promise, has entered the struggle between the two realms.

Lutheranism does not have a good track record when it comes to living in the two realms, but some of the best and brightest Lutherans have been powerful models of such a life. They were able to use the realm of law, the "left hand of God," as a significant bridge between Christians and non-Christians in their joint combat against evil. One does not have to be a Christian to work for peace, justice, a clean environment, and whatever else helps preserve God's creation from sin, evil, and death. The law helps create justice and a proper balance between human arrogance and common sense. Here the chief article of faith, "justification by grace through faith without the works of law," decisively affects Christian ethics. One does not do moral deeds to be saved, to earn the right relationship with God. Such deeds are done in order to create a better world. One is saved by grace *(gratis)*, unconditionally trusting Christ's atonement for our sin, which results in helping one's neighbor. The issue of reward or punishment for moral deeds belongs to the realm of the hidden God. It is God's problem, not ours.

The church, then, is the community that lives in both realms—that of the law with its call for order and that of the gospel—with its promise of a new creation. Lutherans know how difficult it is to live in both realms. They, like other Christians, have been tempted to focus solely on law and order, and at other times to idealize life lived in the gospel.

Christian tradition likes to compare the church to a ship tossed about in the rough seas of the world. Members of the church are not on a pleasure cruise, they are the crew, and are obligated to do everything in their power to keep the ship afloat. The ship is in constant touch with its real captain, Christ. Gathering every seventh day for the past two millennia, Christians have been strengthened in their discipleship by Christ's presence in word and sacrament, liturgy and prayer, and meditation and celebration. But there is always Monday with its struggles between law and gospel. Using another image, the church is a halfway house between the two realms. "Now we are only halfway pure and holy," Luther told his congregation. "The Holy Spirit must continue to work in us through the Word, daily granting forgiveness until we attain to that life where there will be no more [need for] forgiveness" (*BC* 418:58). One must therefore remain vigilant and be able to distinguish properly between sin and grace, law and gospel, and church and world.

This skill of discernment is enhanced and strengthened by the Holy Spirit, Christ's "advocate," who helps disciples survive the meantime, which can be mean and eerie (John 14:26). Sometimes the Holy Spirit bestows specific gifts, "charisms" (from the Greek *charismata*, meaning "gifts of the Spirit"). These gifts range from speaking in tongues to accomplishing acts of selfless love (1 Cor. 12–13). Some charismatic Christians are under the illusion that the Holy Spirit will spare them struggle, doubt, and confusion. Yet even they experience temptation, doubt, and the need to be "born again" more than once.

Lutherans are more realistic, knowing that the struggle between the two realms does not end until the Last Day, the day on which Christ begins his reign. As a consequence of this struggle, the marks of the church include suffering as well as worship, ministry, and love. One example of Lutheran suffering was the experience of some German Lutherans under the tyranny of Adolf Hitler. The Lutheran pastor Dietrich Bonhoeffer (1906–45) demanded that the church remain faithful to Christ and therefore resist the lure of German nationalism. He knew that the church spoke with a forked tongue when it claimed to be loyal to both Christ and Hitler. He made the difficult distinction between "cheap" and "costly" grace. "Cheap grace" means hiding behind rhetoric so one does not have to act. "Costly grace" means putting one's life on the line for Christ, as Dietrich Bonhoeffer did in his failed assassination attempt on Hitler's life in 1945. Christians do not need to become victims of a "messiah complex," hurrying to the cross and volunteering to be crucified, but they should not shy away from suffering if suffering is a result of bearing witness to Christ in the world.

Christians have been entrusted with a mission during the interim between Christ's ascension and his second coming at the end of time. Just before his ascension, Jesus commanded his disciples to make other disciples in all nations by baptizing them and teaching them to observe all that he had commanded. He promised to be with them and their successors on this mission until the last day (Matt. 28:19-20). It took a while for the first disciples to start their mission because they were afraid of being persecuted in a world hostile to Christianity. But Christ's Holy Spirit drove them into the streets of Jerusalem at Pentecost to proclaim the advent of the promised "new age." Peter admonished the astounded listeners, "Save yourselves from the corrupt generation!" (Acts 2:40). As a result, about three thousand people were baptized on that day.

This is how the church was born. The first baptized converts formed a community known as "the body of Christ" and proclaimed the future that had begun with the resurrection of Jesus. Membership in this community was based on one's faith in the resurrected Christ, which was perceived as a gift of God given by the Holy Spirit. The Holy Spirit was the driving force of the active church, later known as "militant," whose members would die and then join the "triumphant church." The church is the visible, corporate community that considers itself to be the extension of the resurrected Jesus because of its power to communicate, "His name is called The Word of God" (Rev. 19:13). The Holy Spirit works through the spoken word, the visible witness of the sacrament of baptism, and other "visible words."

Luther was emphatic about the relationship of the Holy Spirit to word and to faith. He stated, "I believe that by my own reason or strength I cannot believe in Jesus Christ, my Lord, or come to him. But the Holy Spirit has called me through the Gospel" (*BC* 345:6). He added that the Holy Spirit links every single believer to a worldwide church, calling him "just as he calls, gathers, enlightens, and sanctifies the whole Christian church on earth and preserves it in union with

Jesus Christ in the one true faith" (*BC* 345:6). The church, therefore, is a community of truly "spirited" people united with other believers throughout the world regardless of national, geographic, ethnic, or other differences. The church exhibits what the Augsburg Confession calls "the new obedience" (*BC* 31:6). The church's life is governed by faith in Christ alone, rather than by any trust in human merit. Lutheranism lives and dies by the communication of what God has done in Christ, for this Christ-centered communication is the church's only mission in the world. Missionaries only need to worry about this center and not about the success of their communicating. Success belongs to the Holy Spirit, which is why the church is a product of the Holy Spirit rather than the result of purely human efforts, be they schemes of organization, entertainment evangelism, or any other gimmick. To obtain faith in Christ, God created a ministry of word and sacrament as the instrument through which the Spirit works. "The Holy Spirit produces faith where and when it pleases God, in those who hear the Gospel" (*BC* 31:2).

The Holy Spirit is undeniably tied to humans sharing the story of Christ's death and resurrection, but a proper distinction between "Spirit" and "Word" must be maintained. This should give some comfort to the pastors who wish to have their faithfulness matched by success. They need not emulate cattle ranchers who rope, brand, and count their herds, nor need they be Lone Rangers trying to please God by undertaking an individual spiritual marathon. They need only be faithful instruments of the Word of God, functioning as the communicators of law and gospel. What they should worry about is expertise in communication, involving public speaking, grace in liturgy, and making their points clear.

Since Lutheranism views the ministry of the baptized as service through the vocations and callings of its members, pastors should encourage and support the members in their mission to witness to Christ in the world. The ordained and the nonordained constitute a partnership in representing the embodied Word of God in the world. Whether in the ordained public ministry of word and sacrament or in another vocation, faithfulness to ministry means doing one's best. For example, there is no difference between a Christian and a non-Christian teacher, except that a Christian teacher will teach to the utmost of his or her ability. The difference is excellence in serving, not piousness.

◇───◇

Back to the Future

In his Large Catechism, Luther called Christians to return to baptism, and to return to the future that began with their initiation into a life with Christ. He declared, "Repentance, therefore, is nothing else than a return and approach to Baptism, to resume and practice what had earlier been begun but abandoned" (*BC* 446:79). Life in the meantime may become so sordid that one falls away from baptism, in which case one must reaffirm it, return to it, and go back to where the future began.

The rite of baptism, the most ancient of all Christian rites, illustrates the meaning of going back to the future and holding on to it, being born again and again. Luther said that baptism "signifies that the old Adam [and Eve] in us, together with all our sins and evil lusts, should be drowned by daily sorrow and repentance and be put to death, and that the new man [and woman] should come forth daily and rise up, cleansed and righteous, to live forever in God's presence" (*BC* 349:12). The liturgy of baptism begins with the recognition that "we are born children of a fallen humanity; in the waters of baptism we are born children of God and inheritors of eternal life."

Baptism initiates us into a new life with God, who in Christ woos human beings into a future with him. Candidates for baptism should be clearly informed about their future with Christ, and warned about how adventurous such a future will be, for the baptismal liturgy clearly reveals what a new life in Christ involves.

First, baptismal candidates are asked to renounce evil. Tradition calls this first part "exorcism," as it renounces "all the forces of evil, the devil and all his empty promises." Evil, that which is diabolical, is the force which confuses the story of Christ with other stories. Generic "good news" becomes confused with the gospel, which is the good news about Christ. Evil always gets people off balance. Luther told his parishioners that the devil builds a chapel beside the church that is "larger than God's temple," since he wants Christian souls as his final prize. All others are already his.

Next, candidates commit themselves to the faith of the church as summarized in the Apostles' Creed. The trinitarian creeds (Apostolic,

Nicene, Athanasian) affirm that God is in charge of all creation, that Christ has overcome evil, and that the Holy Spirit sustains believers between Christ's first and second coming.

Candidates for baptism are then "sealed by the Holy Spirit and marked with the cross of Christ forever." This liturgical action warns the newly baptized that their lives will be an adventure with Christ, whose spirit has been given them to help them survive the meantime, which may become a truly *mean* time. The lives of the baptized are sealed like an envelope ready to be mailed; and they will remain safe during the pilgrimage of living, though many will suffer. Life in Christ is, after all, like crucifixion. It is lived in solidarity with the crucified Jesus who has borne and atoned for more sin than any human ever will. The church, as symbolized by the "body of Christ," is therefore exposed to struggle, persecution, and even death.

Finally, candidates for baptism are made part of Christ's priesthood, so that "we may proclaim the praise of God and bear his creative and redeeming Word to all the world." The certificate of baptism is comforting evidence that the new birth has begun, but the baptized are assigned to tasks of mission, which means struggle. The struggle between the realm of sin and the realm of faith is real and must be faced every day, which is why one continually needs to be born anew. One is called back to the future, to return to that which was begun in baptism.

Some churches baptize adults only, because they require evidence of faith on the part of the candidate before they will baptize. This evidence is usually in the form of adult confession. Lutherans baptize infants, for no one is too young to be exposed to the power of the future, and the power of the future is embodied in the church, the extension of Christ's presence on earth. However, the promise is given to tell the children of their rebirth and its significance in the church, just as they are told of their birth into a family.

◇────────────────────────────────◇

Servanthood and Serpenthood

The communion of believers exists in space and time as a visible sign of our future with God through Christ. The third article of the Apostles'

Creed speaks of the church as a holy community, whose source is the Holy Spirit. Martin Luther explained the Creed this way: "The Holy Spirit carries on his work unceasingly until the last day. For this purpose, he has appointed a community on earth, through which he speaks and does all his work (*BC* 419:61). In this sense, the church is the "mouth" of the Holy Spirit (rather than a "penhouse"), as Luther was fond of saying. The church, then, is a gathering and an event at which the story of Christ is told and heard until the last day. The Augsburg Confession asserts that "one holy Christian church will be and remain forever" (*BC* 32:7). The church is not any particular denomination, such as Lutheran or Roman Catholic; it exists where the gospel is preached, taught, and enacted sacramentally.

Since "gospelling" is the basic business of the church, the people of God are charged to be faithful servants and to participate in that mission. Lutherans learned from the apostle Paul that this mission is in a world in which Christians are resident aliens, "strangers and foreigners on the earth, ... seeking a homeland" (Heb. 11:13-14). As a result, Lutherans consider the church to be an embassy representing an unknown future to most residents, consider themselves "ambassadors for Christ, since God is making his appeal through us" (2 Cor. 5:20).

Servants of the church also know that there is no such thing as purity of service in this world. The Augsburg Confession calls the church a mixed body of saints and sinners, because "in this life many false Christians, hypocrites, and even open sinners remain among the godly" (*BC* 33). Early Lutheranism was a movement trying to make distinctions between the true and the false church, and the proper use and the abuse of the gospel. People tend to avoid conflict and suffering when it is possible. The church often makes the gospel less offensive to people by compromising its message. But one of the chief consequences of servanthood, carrying out God's mission, is more often conflict and suffering. "The blood of the martyrs is the seed of the church," said the Christians who endured Roman persecutions in the first three centuries. In the New Testament, the word "witness" means "martyr." When Jesus sent out his disciples he told them, "See, I am sending you out like sheep into the midst of wolves; so be wise as serpents and innocent as doves" (Matt. 10:16). The first disciples had to learn what it means to practice both servant- and serpent-hood. There is joy in glorifying God and in being filled with thanksgiving and praise like a cooing dove. Christians should celebrate and make a joyful noise unto the Lord; without such childlike innocence, they remain unreal. But the "church militant" on earth also needs the wisdom of the serpent. Christians must be vigilant—discerning the signs of the times, and, like expert physicians, diagnosing the ills of the world. They will then be able to heal and to accomplish their mission. Paul was a Jew to the Jews and a Gentile to the Gentiles; "I have become all things to all people, that I might by all means save some" (1 Cor. 9:22). In order to reach each other, lovers use much imagination and a little cunning.

There is, however, a fine line between wooing and selling out. Sometimes one must exercise "tough love," insisting on what is good for the beloved even when the beloved rejects it. The serpent is the symbol of medicine; surgery is the exercising of tough love on the physical body. In hospital trauma stations and emergency rooms, one does what is necessary to save a life, according to hard and consistent lifesaving training, and without asking for a vote among the patient and the patient's family as to procedure. Human reason is the basis of this kind of love. One does not administer first aid to someone in need just because one feels like it; one only does so after learning how through practice and first aid classes. Doctors are most successful when they act as cold-blooded, rational technicians who do what is necessary. For this reason they usually refuse to treat their loved ones.

The serpenthood of the saints is very often rational cold-bloodedness for the sake of caring for the neighbor. The wisdom of the serpent accompanies reading the signs of the times (one must know how to assess and discern a situation). Luther was a good serpent; he was well trained to discern the abuses in the church of his time. But he could also be gentle when he encountered the weak and the uneducated. Consequently he was a hard-hitting theologian when he faced Rome, and a wise pastor when he faced his parishioners in Wittenberg.

Lutherans have therefore learned to appreciate both the qualities of servanthood and serpenthood in mission. Well-equipped saints are attractive to others, and saints must be attractive if they wish to participate in God's worldly mission. This means, first of all, that they must be recognized as real human beings, as what Germans call *Mensch*. They are trustworthy, wise, committed, and have a sense of humor (like "a court jester," as Luther called himself), and are willing to be "fools for the sake of Christ ... [and] wise in Christ" (1 Cor. 4:10). The ideal

Lutheran pastor is like a rabbi: well schooled, wise in the ways of suffering and meditation, always ready to communicate, a wooer with a lifelong commitment to the ministry and a trusted servant with a serpentine mind who looks for new ways to proclaim life with God.

Servanthood rehumanizes what has been dehumanized in the world, and serpenthood exorcises the legion of demons feeding the inhumanity in the world. The church, too, must be rehumanized. As a human institution, it is tempted to forget how thoroughly human God was in Jesus; it tries to remove God from humanity, creating a God of convenience, or a far-off God on the throne. The church, too, falls into the "original sin" of trying to "be like God," that is, of disobeying the first commandment of the decalogue, "I . . . am your God, . . . you shall have no other gods before me" (Exod. 20:2-3). The church is dehumanized when it deifies dogma, structure, morality, or any other human invention. It forgets that God in Christ "emptied himself" and became human, "obedient to the point of death," in order to demonstrate what "the body of Christ" on earth should be (Phil. 2:7-8).

Like skilled physicians, disciples must learn to treat the diseases of Christ's body on earth. They must sometimes be doctors of theology who know when and where to operate on the church to keep it healthy. Jesus transformed the ancient symbol of evil, the serpent, into the image of Christian vigilance and wisdom, for "just as Moses lifted up the serpent in the wilderness, so must the Son of Man be lifted up, that whoever believes in him may have eternal life" (John 3:14). Lutheranism knows the proper balance between servanthood, a childlike faith, and serpenthood, the vigilance to detect and the wisdom to combat evil. Vigilance is the price of liberty.

Lutheranism was born under ecclesiastical tyranny and has fought for Christian liberty in the name of the Gospel. Thus Lutherans must now remind the whole "church militant" that room must be made in the church to accommodate both the innocent doves and the wise serpents until the day that "Christ is all and in all" (Col. 3:11).

Formation for Mission

Worship

Luther defined worship in its deepest sense as complete trust in God. "To have God, you see, does not mean to lay hands on him, or put him into a purse, or shut him up in a chest. To cling to him with all our heart is nothing else than to entrust ourselves to him completely" (*BC* 366:13–15). True worship is unreserved faith in God. False worship is self-righteous religiosity. According to Luther, false worship "concerns only that conscience which seeks help, comfort, and salvation in its own works and presumed to wrest heaven from God" (*BC* 367:22). At issue is obedience to God's first commandment, "You shall have no other gods."

From the very beginning, Lutheranism viewed public worship as the celebration of Christ's presence with his people, especially in the Lord's Supper. Unlike other reformers (Ulrich Zwingli and John Calvin in Switzerland), Luther did not abolish the Mass. Lutheran reformers told their Catholic opponents that "in our churches Mass is celebrated every Sunday and on other festivals" (*BC* 249:1). Lutheran public worship kept traditional liturgical forms, vestments, and the ancient designation of the Mass as "sacrifice of praise" (*BC* 253:25). Liturgical reform centered in clear communication. It used vernacular language, well-rehearsed liturgy, and effective preaching. Since baptism commissions believers to ministry, every member of the congregation participates in public worship, be it by singing, reading Scripture lessons, or assisting at Holy Communion. Such participation requires instruction and rehearsal so that everything is done in harmony and good order.

Luther linked Sunday worship with rest after the labors of the week. One liturgy is the Sunday liturgy, "the work of the people" (from the Greek *"leiturgia,"* meaning "public duties"). This liturgy culminates in the thanksgiving celebration of the Eucharist (from the Greek *"eucharistia*—thanksgiving"). Luther described Sundays and festivals in the Christian calendar as *"Feiertage,"* or days of rest and holy days (from *"feiern,"* meaning "to celebrate, take time off from work"). Luther also used this word in interpreting the third commandment of the decalogue, "Remember the Sabbath day, to keep it holy."

> God set apart the seventh day and appointed it for rest. . . . What is meant by "keeping it holy"? Nothing else than to devote it to holy words, holy works, holy life. In itself the day needs no sanctification, for it was created holy. But God wants it to be holy to you. So it becomes holy or unholy on your account, according as you spend the day in doing holy or unholy things.
>
> (*BC* 375:80, 376–77:87).

Sanctifying takes place "when we occupy ourselves with God's Word and exercise ourselves in it" (*BC* 377:88). God's word comes as law and gospel. The law reveals sin (Rom. 3:20), and exposes our inability to do what God commands. The gospel is the good news that Christ atoned for human sin and that faith in him restores the broken relationship with God. "At whatever time God's Word is taught, preached, heard, read, or pondered, there the person, the day, and the work are sanctified by it" (*BC* 377:92).

Lutheran books of worship regulate worship by offering liturgical settings for spiritual direction and discipline. They include Holy Communion, a service of the word when there is no eucharist, morning and evening prayers, orders for public and private confessions, baptism and funeral liturgies, psalms, prayers, creeds, daily readings from Scripture, and hymns. In addition, there are companion books for occasional services, including Holy Communion in special circumstances (for the

sick and dying), marriage, ordination and installation of pastors, com-
missioning of lay leaders, dedication of buildings and cemeteries, re-
ception of new members, and even guidelines for ringing church bells.

At the center of worship is the celebration of the gospel, the promise
of a future with God for those who trust in Christ alone. The gospel

> offers counsel and help against sin in more than one way, for God is
> surpassingly rich in his grace: First through the spoken word, by which
> forgiveness of sin (the peculiar function of the Gospel) is preached to the
> whole world; second, through Baptism, third, through the holy Sacrament
> of the Altar; fourth, through the power of keys [confession and absolution];
> and finally, through the mutual conversation and consolation of [brothers
> and sisters].
>
> (BC 310:4).

Post-reformation Lutheran worship meant to offer a proper balance
between ceremony and the daily flow of Christian life. There was to
be a preservation of the best of the liturgical tradition, especially in the
celebration of the Mass. But more often than not, both clergy and laity
ignored Luther's call for a reformed restoration of the ancient liturgical
tradition. As a result, the order of the Mass gave way to bland, wordy
services, reflecting the influence of the Swiss reformation with its lack
of ceremony and music. The presiding minister would wear a black
robe instead of the white alb, the service was somber, and Holy Communion was celebrated only four times a year (the custom instituted
by Zwingli in Zurich), or only on certain Sundays. Holy Communion
became linked to the confession of sin and had a funereal character.
The popular movement of Pietism in Germany and Scandinavia linked
confirmation to Holy Communion, thus prohibiting children younger
than fourteen to commune. The alternative to such Sunday services was
often an emphasis on pomp and ceremony, without much participation
of the laity. Clericalized "chancel prancing" segregated clergy and laity,
and the connection between liturgy and life was lost.

Worship is the most significant part of the instrumentation of the
gospel. The major responsibility for this instrumentation is placed on
the ordained minister whose office is instituted by God to provide word
and sacrament. "For through the Word and the sacraments, as through
instruments, the Holy Spirit is given, and the Holy Spirit produces

faith, where and when it pleases God, in those who hear the Gospel" (*BC* 31:2). Presiding ministers are to concentrate on how they lead worship rather than how worship creates believers. Faith is a gift of the Holy Spirit that "blows where it chooses" (John 3:8). This ought to be a consolation to pastors who burn out over the question whether anyone believers them.

Lutheran worship is communal and the Holy Spirit uses word and sacrament to add new members. Luther writes: "I was brought to [the church] by the Holy Spirit and incorporated into it through the fact that I have heard and still hear God's Word, which is the first step in entering it" (*BC* 417:52). The church is the community through which God does the work of redemption for all of humankind. "Creation is past and redemption is accomplished," Luther writes, "but the Holy Spirit carries on his work unceasingly until the last day. For this purpose he has appointed a community on earth, through which he speaks and does all his work" (*BC* 419:61).

Worship is the lifeline of the church to Christ, its head. All members of the body of Christ (the church) are under his direction. Worship is the heartbeat of the church. The strength of the beat determines what the body can do. The church as the body of Christ has a mission to the world: to baptize and make disciples who follow Jesus (Matt. 28:19-20). Worship is the key to formation for mission.

Education

Worship and education are the twin pillars of the church. Luther combined liturgical with catechetical reforms so that clergy and laity could be partners in ministry.

Lutheran Christian education trains for life in community, in the church. The church is the embodiment of the gospel in a world plagued by evil, sin, and death. Evil is the mysterious force that divides and confuses (related to "diabolical" from the Greek *diaballein*, meaning "to tear apart"). Sin is the temptation to be like God (Gen. 3:5). Death is the shadow that darkens all of life.

The Lutheran catechisms have five parts: the Ten Commandments, the Apostles' Creed, the Lord's Prayer, Baptism, and the Lord's Supper. These five parts portray life in the church, foreshadowing a life without evil, sin, and death with God in the future.

The first of the Ten Commandments sets the tone for Christian education: trust in God alone. "Learn from these words, then," Luther writes, "how angry God is with those who rely on anything but himself, and again, how gracious he is to those who trust and believe him alone with their whole heart" (*BC* 369:31–32). The Apostles' Creed shows how God cares for the world, how in Christ he promises a new life without sin, and how the church is guided by the Holy Spirit in the interim between Christ's first and second coming. Every member of the church is connected with every other member around the world (*BC* 345:6). They are connected with Christ through prayer, especially the Lord's Prayer. They begin their life in the church through baptism, and they are sustained in their pilgrimage by the Lord's Supper, the "daily food" (*BC* 449:24).

Luther's Catechisms ("Small" meaning for children and "Large" for adults; from the Greek *katechein*, meaning "echoing, learning by oral instruction") are blueprints for an educational program designed to discern the distinction between earthly life and the life promised by the gospel.

To illustrate: the Ten Commandments regulate life in the family and with neighbours outside the family. Relationships must be guided by honest communication and mutual respect. But there are the "sins of the tongue," a violation of the eighth commandment ("You shall not bear false witness against your neighbor"). "Backbiters" use gossip, "relishing and delighting in it like pigs that roll in the mud and root around in it with their snouts. This is nothing else than usurping the judgement and office of God" (*BC* 401:267–68).

In the face of evil and temptation, one must learn to pray to God as Jesus taught: "Lead us not into temptation, but deliver us from evil." Only prayer keeps evil at bay. "Otherwise, if you attempt to help yourself by your own thoughts and counsels, you will only make the matter worse and give the devil a better opening" (*BC* 435:111).

Lutheran catechetical instruction is pragmatic. At its best, it creates a style of life that models the tension between the old life of sin and the new life promised by the gospel. Baptism is the entrance into this struggle between the old and the new. One lives in penance, with "a change of mind" (from the Greek for *metanoia*, meaning "penance"), promised by the gospel through the power of the Holy Spirit.

Luther writes, "If you live in repentance, therefore, you are walking in Baptism, which not only announces this new life but also produces, begins, and promotes it" (*BC* 445:75). Luther called all of life a return to baptism, "the daily garment" which one must "wear all the time" (*BC* 446:83–84).

Life after baptism is nurtured in the community of believers who confess their sins to each other and absolve each other from sin with the mutual promise of the gospel, the good news that there is a new life in Christ. That is why "going to confession" is part of the rhythm of Christian life. As Luther put it: "When I urge you to go to confession, I am simply urging you to be a Christian" (*BC* 460:31–32).

In Luther's time there was still a Christian culture. Going to confession was like going to a trusted therapist today. Doing penance in this manner was part of sacramental nurture. That is why penance was called the third sacrament (*BC* 211:4; 445:74). Luther linked it with baptism rather than the Lord's Supper, as the medieval Roman Catholic Church had done since 1215 A.D., when going to confession at age seven became the condition for admission to the Lord's Supper. The Eastern Orthodox Church maintained the ancient sacramental nurture with a threefold act of initiation consisting of baptism, communion, and confirmation. Even infants were so initiated (being anointed with holy oil as a sign of "confirmation"). Frequently going to confession and to the Lord's Supper was the continuation of sacramental nurture. Although Luther did not revive the ancient tradition of infant communion, he did encourage the communion of children. "Since they are baptized and received into the Christian church, they should also enjoy this fellowship of the sacrament" (*BC* 456:87). Eighteenth-century Lutheran Pietism increased the distance between infant baptism and Holy Communion when it made confirmation the condition for admission to the Lord's Supper, usually at age fourteen, thus doubling the age introduced by Rome. Some Lutheran catechisms even taught that infant baptism is one half of the sacrament of baptism and confirmation is the other half.

If Lutheranism is to remain true to its historical roots, it must restore the sacramental and educational initiation into the church and its own "culture," and even counterculture. Thus parents need extensive pre-baptismal counseling in order to be able to keep the promises made at the baptism of their children: to bring them to worship, to teach them the catechism, to study the Holy Scriptures, and to make them faithful members of the church. Families need to learn and enjoy singing Christian hymns, know the stories of the Bible, understand Christian doctrine, and become witnesses to Christ in word and deed. At a time of religious pluralism, the church is like a Christian island in the sea of a post-Christian world. Education for life on the island begins with sacramental nurture by baptism and Holy Communion, combined with a theological curriculum geared to various stages of growth. Confirmation concludes the first, most essential part of Christian education. Then follows the churchly life of continuing education, leading to disciplined discipleship undergirded by worship. A three-step program recommends itself to Lutherans who stand in a tradition of continual reform. Such reform is begun with the formation of a cadre of one-tenth of the active members of the congregation, a living "tithe," as it were.

1. Led by their pastor, the cadre meets at least weekly for intensive study of essential Christian teachings, based on Scripture and the Lutheran tradition. Basic issues and answers should surface in these sessions through a pragmatic use of resources, active listening, and informed discussion. Each session should include prayer and conclude with the celebration of the Lord's Supper.

2. In the first year, attempts should begin to reshape the program of Christian education, using the insights and findings of the cadre. Adult forums, or similar teaching events, should deal with essential Christian teaching, the Lutheran legacy, and questions arising out of community experiences. In this way, members of the congregation are wooed into joining the cadre's efforts toward renewal.

3. The congregation should consider all other congregations in the community as allies rather than competitors. Common educational goals can be established, even though congregations and churches have not yet experienced full communion, sharing altars

and pulpits. But they can develop educational programs, such as vacation Bible schools or forums dealing with problems in the community. Thus Christian education becomes an indispensable part of the congregational formation for mission.

Ethics

Lutheranism teaches that faith without moral action is dead. Moral action is termed "doing good works."

> Good works should and must be done, not that we are to rely on them to earn grace but that we may do God's will and glorify him. It is always faith alone that apprehends grace and forgiveness of sin. When through faith the Holy Spirit is given, the heart is moved to do good works.
>
> (*BC* 45:27–30)

But believers are caught in a dilemma: even though they try to do their best "good works," they are unable to succeed because of an innate desire not to do good. As the apostle Paul put it: "I can will what is right, but I cannot do it. For I do not do the good I want, but the evil I do not want is what I do" (Rom. 7:18b-19). The innate evil is the temptation to be like God (Gen. 3:5).

One must be born again to a new obedience in the midst of this dilemma. Life must be grounded in faith alone. In Luther's words: "Faith is a divine work in us that transforms us and begets us anew from God, kills the old Adam [and Eve], makes us entirely different people in heart, spirit, mind, and all our powers, and brings the Holy Spirit with it" (*BC* 552:10). Christian ethics is the life of faith with the power of the Holy Spirit sanctifying "good works." There are no revealed ethical norms about the various situations of earthly life. There is only faithful obedience to the God who creates a new and everlasting relationship with humanity through Christ and the Holy Spirit.

Good works, then, do not merit God's love. They are the fruits of the Holy Spirit, the power which makes faith come alive in love. Luther learned this basic insight from the apostle Paul who told his congregation in Rome that one "is justified by faith apart from the works prescribed by the law" (Rom. 3:28). If one tries to do good according to the law, one will despair because one can never do enough to appease God for the innate sin of disobedience.

Since humans are justified before God by faith "apart from works of the law," our "good works" have no merit for ourselves. We do them in obedience to God who has called us to be "co-workers" in the world until Christ comes again (1 Cor. 3:9). Like the good Samaritan, we must care for the neighbor in need (Luke 10:30-37); not to look good to others and ourselves, but to balance self-love with love of neighbor (Luke 10:27). This is the most elementary form of justice and love of neighbor because doing something for another cancels self-love.

Lutheran ethics is "situation ethics": every situation is an occasion to embody faith in the love of neighbor, be it a person in need, family, government, or any other relationships. Such love is kind and tough; it cuts the nerve of egocentricity. Why be a good Samaritan? Because God says it is good to be one, not because there is virtue or reward in being good. Why do I help the victim on the road? So that he or she is helped. Why should he or she be helped? So that he or she can have a sound body for God's resurrection.

Life with the gospel is shaped by the call for a radically new moral stance: "Be transformed by the renewing of your minds, so that you may discern what is the will of God—what is good and acceptable and perfect" (Rom 12:2).

Lutheran ethics are consoling for those who worry about the consequences of their actions, for questions of reward and punishment are no longer on the agenda of Christian morality. There is only "the crown of righteousness" shared with Christ in eternity (2 Tim. 4:8). But disciples of Christ cannot regard this promise as an "incentive to work for their own advantage, since they should work for the glory of God. But to escape despair amid afflictions, they should know that it is the will of God to help, rescue, and save them" (BC 162–63:364).

This basic Lutheran ethical stance has not been well nurtured in Lutheranism. Lutherans have joined other denominations in their retreat from such basic ethical Reformation insights. They sided with those who think that a divine code of morals links ethics to eternal reward and punishment. Lutherans have made an ethical investment in the notion of unchangeable "orders of creation," such as marriage, family, and government. This view had dire consequences because it led Lutherans to believe that one must obey all forms of governments, even tyranny. The Augsburg Confession, however, sets limits to political obedience: "All government in the world and all established rule and laws were instituted and ordained by God for the sake of good order, and that Christians may without sin occupy civil offices. . . . But when commands of the civil authority cannot be obeyed without sin, we must obey God rather than [humans]" (Acts 5:29) (*BC* 37:1–2; 38:7).

Lutheran ethics is anchored in discipleship to Christ who leads the church during the interim between Christ's ascension and return. Thus Christian ethics is an "interim ethics." It liberates the mind from anxiety over reward and punishment and for full concentration on the Christian mission in the world. The good Samaritan offers selfless help to the victim. A bad Samaritan would offer egocentric charity, or would tell the victim, "Whoever did this to you needs a lot of help."

There is the "glorious liberty of the children of God" (Rom. 8:21, an. trans.), but the price of such liberty is eternal vigilance against moral egocentricity. At times, this stance will lead to suffering because the world (and some churches) will not tolerate it. But the way of the cross is a familiar part of Christian faith and life.

The Gift of Unity

Scripture and Tradition

The Lutheran reform movement of the sixteenth century was ecumenical, not sectarian. It labored for unity under the word of God and refused to be labelled "Lutheran"—a designation used by Roman Catholic opponents since 1519. The Augsburg Confession was submitted to Emperor Charles V in 1530 "as the common confession of the reformed churches," also known as "symbol" or one of the "symbolical writings" in *The Book of Concord*. Adherents to these "reformed churches," which had been established in certain German territories, were also known as "evangelicals" (from the German *die Evangelischen*, meaning "gospellers," or "people of the gospel"). According to *The Book of Concord*,

> [The Augsburg Confession] distinguishes our reformed churches from the papacy and from other condemned sects and heresies. We appeal to it just as in the ancient church it was traditional and customary for later synods and Christian bishops and teachers to appeal and confess adherence to the Nicene Creed."
>
> (*BC* 504:5)

The Augsburg Confession wanted to remove abuses from the church rather than split the church. The issue was the preservation of Christian

teaching "which agrees with the pure Word of God and Christian truth."
Such teaching "is grounded clearly in the Holy Scriptures and is not
contrary or opposed to that of the universal Christian church, or even
the Roman church (insofar as the latter's teaching is reflected in the
writings of the Fathers [of the ancient church in the West]" (*BC* 47:1).
This is why *The Book of Concord* has an appendix (in the original
German and Latin editions) entitled "Catalogue of Testimonies From
Holy Scripture and the Ancient Pure Teachers of the Church").

The "word of God," proclaimed as divine judgement on sin and as
promise of forgiveness through Christ, is the final norm of the church.
"We pledge ourselves to the prophetic and apostolic writings of the Old
and New Testaments as the pure and clear fountain of Israel, which is
the only true norm according to which all teachers and teachings are
to be judged and evaluated (*BC* 503–504:3). "The true Christian doctrine," the essential tradition, is summarized in "the three catholic or
ecumenical symbols" or "drawn together out of God's Word" (*BC* 17;
504:4).

Scripture and the trinitarian creeds affirm Christ as the incarnate
word of God (John 1:14) in whom God accounts as righteous those
who rely on Christ alone.

> We must not trust that we are accounted righteous before God by our own
> perfection and keeping of the law, but only because of Christ.
>
> This is so because, first of all, Christ does not stop being the mediator
> after our renewal. It is an error to suppose [as medieval theology did] that
> he merely merited "initial grace" and that afterward we please God and
> merit eternal life by our keeping of the law. Christ remains the mediator.
> We must always be sure that for his sake we have a gracious God in spite
> of our unworthiness.
>
> (*BC* 129:161–163).

One must distinguish between Scripture and the essential gospel
tradition on the one hand, and the means by which the gospel is
transmitted to later generations on the other. These means are language,
liturgy, polity, or "church usages" and "ecclesiastical rites" (as the Augsburg Confession calls them [*BC* 36:15]). Whatever the means, they
constitute "the human tradition" through which the word of God is
communicated. "Church usages" such as holy days or church consti-

tutions "contribute to peace and good order in the church," but "consciences may not be burdened by the notion that such things are necessary for salvation" (BC 36:15, 1–2). Lutherans, therefore, did not abolish traditions that are not explicitly mentioned in the Bible, such as the liturgy of the Mass, various ways to organize the church, or specific rules of conduct in a post-biblical world. "We gladly keep the old traditions set up in the church because they are useful and promote tranquility, and we interpret them in an evangelical way, excluding the opinion which holds that they justify" (BC 220:38). Thus Lutheranism has kept the tradition of episcopal order, not because God wants only bishops to lead the church, but because they have created an honorable and effective way of governing the church through the ages. They are ordained ministers with a special call for supervision. But when they abuse their power they must be replaced by a better "human tradition." As Luther put it:

> If the bishops were true bishops and were concerned about the church and the Gospel, they might be permitted (for the sake of love and unity, but not of necessity) to ordain and confirm us and our preachers, provided this can be done without pretense, humbug, and unchristian ostentation.
>
> (BC 314:10, 1)

Philipp Melanchthon, Luther's valuable colleague and author of the Augsburg Confession, was very eager to preserve unity with Rome. He was even willing to accept the authority of the papacy, if it were understood as part of a good "human tradition." He writes:

> Concerning the pope, I hold that, if he would allow the Gospel, we, too, may concede to him that superiority over the bishops which he possesses by human right, making this concession for the sake of peace and general unity among the Christians who are now under him and who may be in the future.
>
> (BC 316–17)

The Bible norms the post-biblical tradition because God discloses "the two chief works" in humankind: to terrify through the law and to console through the gospel.

> One or the other of these works is spoken of throughout Scripture. One part is the law, which reveals, denounces, and condemns sin. The other

part is the Gospel, that is, the promise of grace granted in Christ. This promise is repeated continually throughout Scripture; first it was given to Adam, later to the patriarchs, then illumined by the prophets, and finally proclaimed and revealed by Christ among the Jews, and spread by the apostles throughout the world. For all the saints were justified by faith in this promise, not by their own attrition or contrition.

(*BC* 189:53–54).

Scripture is authoritative because it reveals the judgement and mercy of God in the life, death, and resurrection of Jesus Christ. Discipleship with Christ is the only way to restore the relationship with God, lost through the sin of disobedience. The Bible is not authoritative in a literal sense; it is not a book of divine rules for all occasions of life. Rather, the Bible is the record of the history of salvation, beginning with Adam and Eve and ending with the second advent of Christ. *The Book of Concord* rejects a biblical fundamentalism which regards every word or story as divinely dictated. Confessional Lutherans do, however, assert the inspiration of Scripture as the record of God's mighty acts among his people. This record lifts up the people of Israel as the nation that harbors the Messiah, Christ, in whom all nations are called to be people of God. Why Israel does not accept Christ is part of the mystery of God, the God who may reserve judgement until the end of human history (Rom. 11:25).

Tradition (from the Latin *tradere*, meaning "handing on") is the process of transmitting the biblical story and promise of salvation in Christ. The method and content of transmission has become complex, controverted, and confusing in the two millennia since Christ's resurrection. Lutheranism has preserved much of the post-biblical tradition based on the stipulation that all human tradition must focus on Christ as the only mediator between God and humankind (1 Tim. 2:5).

The stance regarding "saints" is a case in point. Should deceased saints be remembered in worship? If so, how? By asking them for help in time of trouble? Does Mary, "the God-bearer" (from the Greek *theotokos*, an ancient title of reverence) play a special role in the invocation of saints? The Lutheran Confessions make a clear distinction between the role of Christ and the place of Mary or the saints in the history of salvation: Saints should be honored by giving thanks for what they did while alive; their example strengthens the faith of the living, and their faith should be imitated, especially in one's earthly vocation (*BC* 229:4–5; 230:6). Mary should be honored as "the most blessed virgin" *(laudatissima virgo)*. "She is truly the mother of God and yet remained a virgin" (*BC* 595:24). Luther believed, as much tradition about Mary holds, that she remained a virgin *(semper virgo, (BC* 292, n.3). But Lutherans assert: "We dare not trust in the transfer of the saints' merits to us, as though God were reconciled to us or accounted us righteous or saved us on this account. We obtain the forgiveness of sins only by Christ's merits when we believe in him (*BC* 233:29). Mary may pray for us, but "even though she is worthy of the highest honors, she does not want to be put on the same level as Christ but to have her example considered and followed" (*BC* 232:27).

Scripture and tradition are the means by which Christians are united in their earthly witness. They should communicate the word of God in what they think, say, and do. This communication becomes powerful and effective through the Holy Spirit, the gift of true Christian unity. "God has caused the Word to be published and proclaimed, in which he has given the Holy Spirit to offer and apply to us this treasure of salvation" (*BC* 415:38).

◇———————————————————————◇

Word and Sacrament

The Lutheran reform movement in the sixteenth century tried hard to prevent a schism in the church, even though Luther had been condemned by church and state. Philipp Melanchthon was the principal advocate for a dialogue designed to preserve Christian unity. He had succeeded in maintaining contacts with Catholic officials even after the Augsburg Confession had been rejected in 1530. In 1541, a dialogue team met in Regensburg, Germany, consisting of three Lutherans led by Melanchthon and three Catholics led by Cardinal Caspar Contarini. Emperor Charles V sponsored the meeting; Luther and Pope Paul III tolerated it. After a month of intensive work, the team agreed to regard the Augsburg Confession's reform proposals as legitimate, including its major proposal for reform which stated that at the center of the church's mission is faith in Christ's merits rather than any merit on the part of believers. Believers do "good works" in his name through the power of the Holy Spirit. Though good works do not earn salvation, they contribute to spiritual growth when faith is active in love through the power of the Holy Spirit, who dwells in the faithful and inspires the human decision toward good.

Luther and Rome rejected the Regensburg agreement. Luther did not tolerate any reference to human cooperation with the Holy Spirit, which the Regensburg team had cautiously affirmed. Rome contended that only a formal meeting of bishops called by the pope, called an ecumenical council, could decide matters in dispute. The Council of Trent (1545–63) preserved Catholic unity by removing many abuses. However, the Lutheran reform movement had no voice at Trent. After the Council of Trent, Rome refrained from further dialogue with Lutherans until the conclusion of the Second Vatican Council in 1965 when a bilateral dialogue was initiated in Baltimore. It paved the way for other dialogues on national and international levels.

Article VII of the Augsburg Confession clearly states the Lutheran stance regarding efforts toward a visible unity with other Christians.

> Our churches teach that one holy church is to continue forever. The church is the assembly of saints in which the Gospel is taught purely and the sacraments are administered rightly. For the true unity of the church it is enough to agree concerning the teaching of the Gospel and the administration of the sacraments. It is not necessary that human traditions or rites and ceremonies, instituted by humans, should be alike everywhere.
>
> (BC 32:1–4)

Word and sacrament constitute the unity of the church, wherever it may be, for the church is the "body of Christ" and is present through the gospel which promises a future free from sin and death. The gospel is the audible word in proclamation and the visible word in sacramental enactment. The sacrament is not an addition to proclamation, but is its embodiment in a baptismal washing, and in a meal, the Lord's Supper.

> As the Word enters through the ears to strike the heart, so the rite itself enters through the eyes to move the heart. The Word and the rite have the same effect, for the rite is received by the eyes and is a sort of picture of the Word, signifying the same thing as the Word. Therefore both have the same effect.
>
> (BC 212:5)

When the gospel is proclaimed purely and the sacraments are administered rightly among Christians, unity is achieved. Unity is not uniformity in teaching, government, liturgy or any other human arrangement by churches charged with the mission of the gospel. Christian unity exists when churches can do word and sacrament together—"purely" and "rightly." They do so when they call for faith in Christ alone, and when they celebrate the sacraments according to the scriptural command. This means that Lutherans and other Christians have to do theological homework together in order to discover and agree on a "pure" proclamation and "right" administration of the sacraments. Once they agree on that, they may then make other appropriate arrangements for their mission in the world.

There has been an enduring debate among Lutherans regarding the meaning of "pure" and "right." Some have linked the meaning of these words with a thought structure or a dogmatic system. Consequently, the gospel is communicated as a body of knowledge, a rational "word," or a "sacrament" grounded in doctrine. But the Lutheran Confessions do not view the communication of the gospel as the transmission of a systematic theology or of doctrines made visible in sacraments. Rather, they view the gospel as God's means "which offers counsel and help against sin in more than one way" (BC 310:4), audibly in proclamation and visibly in sacramental celebration. In the case of the latter, the focus is on use or performance rather than on doctrinal understanding (BC 35:13).

The points in negotiations for Christian unity is a belief that Christ alone saves from sin and death, and in the performance of sacraments rather than on doctrines about them. All other ecumenical arrangements are secondary.

Authority and Adiaphora

Lutheranism rediscovered the biblical understanding of the church as a pilgrim in time, made up of "aliens and exiles" (1 Peter 2:11), who are people of "the Way" (Acts 24:14). Like Abraham and his people,

Christians are "strangers and foreigners on the earth," seeking "a better country, that is, a heavenly one" (Heb. 11:13, 16).

The church has its origin in its charge to mission. This is its "authority" (from the Latin *auctoritas*, meaning "origination"). The mission is to communicate the mighty acts of God in the world, beginning with the story of Israel and ending with the ministry of Jesus Christ. All talk of authority, therefore, is talk about communication. When one person addresses another with the story of God's salvation in Christ, the authority of the word of God enters in, both as law and as gospel. As law, God's authority enters in when one is reminded that all attempts to appease God by ego power fail, those attempts only reveal the illusion about the reality of sin. As gospel, the authority of God's Word manifests itself when one is wooed into unconditional faith in Christ who embodied the unconditional love of God for a fallen creation. "For God so loved the world that he gave his only Son, so that everyone who believes in him may not perish but may have eternal life" (John 3:16). The communication of law is conditional: "If you do this, then such and such will happen to you." The communication of the gospel is unconditional: "Because you are who you are, I love you without reservations." One makes a commitment to his or her neighbor, showing them that everyone has a future together by telling of a life beyond death. In this sense, Christ is proclaimed.

Such communication creates the assembly of believers which relies on Christ alone in the struggles of life and maintains contact with him as the head of the church. Christ gives his disciples power. He says, "If two of you agree on earth about anything you ask, it will be done for you by my Father in heaven. For where two or three are gathered in my name, I am there among them" (Matt 18:19-20). Christ is the only authority and power in the church, "and the gates of Hades [hell] will not prevail against it" (Matt 16:18). The Augsburg Confession teaches "that one holy Christian church will be and remain forever" (*BC* 32:7, 1).

The authority of the church, therefore, is grounded in the mission to communicate the gospel and proclaim that a new and never-ending relationship with God has begun in Christ for those who stake their lives on him. When they gather in worship they remember Christ crucified and commit themselves to his mission in the world. They become the church as "the assembly of saints among whom the Gospel is taught purely and the sacraments are administered rightly" (*BC* 32:7, 1–2). Christ is with them in power when they tell of his life, death and resurrection; when they baptize with water in the name of the triune God; and when they celebrate Christ's presence in bread and wine. The communication of the gospel in word and sacrament is essential for salvation. For in such communication Jesus promised to be present. Christ alone is essential. That is why the Lutheran Confessions distinguish between the authority of the word of God and matters which are not essential for salvation, but are necessary for the communication of the word of God. Such matters are language, liturgy, aspects of tradition and the like. They are "matters of indifference" (from the Greek *adiaphora*, meaning "things in the middle"). Adiaphora are "church rites which are neither commanded nor forbidden in the Word of God but which have introduced into the church with good intentions for the sake of good order and decorum or else to preserve Christian discipline" (*BC* 610:10, 1).

Sixteenth-century Lutherans debated the issue of the difference between the authority of the word of God in Scripture and tradition and adiaphora. Some Lutherans kept Roman Catholic practices in worship, doctrine, and moral discipline. Others rejected such adiaphora as being contrary to the gospel. The Lutheran Confessions tried to settle the debate by two assertions. The first was that

> the community of God in every place and at every time has the right, authority, and power to change, to reduce, or to increase ceremonies according to its circumstances, as long as it does so without frivolity and offense but in an orderly and appropriate way, as at any time may seem to be more profitable, beneficial, and salutary for good order, Christian discipline, evangelical decorum, and the edification of the church.
>
> (*BC* 612:9)

There is freedom in regard to the ways in which the church goes about the task of witness and mission in the world. For the church is an interim gathering around word and sacrament, existing in the meantime between Christ's first and second advents. This is why the details regarding witness and mission are left to human ingenuity and are not spelled out by the word of God. Liturgy, doctrine, and discipline are penultimate. The second assertion holds that at a time of confession *[in statu confessionis]*, as when enemies of the Word of God desire to suppress the pure doctrine of the holy Gospel, the entire community of God, yes, every individual Christian, and especially the ministers of the Word as the leaders of the community of God, are obligated to confess openly, not only by words but also through their deeds and actions, the true doctrine and all that pertains to it, according to the Word of God. In such a case we should not yield to adversaries even in matters of indifference, nor should we tolerate the imposition of such ceremonies on us by adversaries in order to undermine the genuine worship of God and to introduce and confirm their idolatry by force or chicanery.

(*BC* 612:10)

One example of this kind of imposition is making the sign of the cross. To Lutherans, it is a matter of Christian liberty, even though crossing oneself is an ancient custom which serves as a reminder of baptism. Under normal conditions, one may or may not make the sign of the cross, but at a time of persecution, when one can only move one's finger, making the sign of the cross is a "time of confession" (*status confessionis*); it is the gospel proclaimed "purely" because there is no other way of doing so.

For here we are no longer dealing with the external adiaphora which in their nature and essence are and remain of themselves free and which accordingly are not subject either to a command or a prohibition, requiring us to use them or to discontinue them. Here we are dealing primarily with the chief article of our Christian faith, so that, as the apostle testifies, the truth of the Gospel might be preserved (Gal. 2:5).

(*BC* 613:14)

There has been an enduring Lutheran debate about the meaning of adiaphorist freedom. What is truly necessary for the mission of the church? What must be done at times when the church is not persecuted? How much long-range planning for mission needs to be considered in the face of an interim existence that might end suddenly with the second advent of Christ? "For you yourselves know very well that the day of the Lord will come like a thief in the night" (1 Thess. 5:2). Sixteenth-century Lutherans viewed much of the accumulated ecclesiastical tradition in the Roman Catholic Church as abused adiaphora: human tradition became confused with the word of God. Church leaders "demand greater strictness in the observance of their traditions than of the Gospel." (*BC* 281:3). But abuse does not eliminate use. That is why Lutheranism regarded human traditions as good adiaphora serving the mission of the gospel. "The holy Fathers did not institute any traditions for the purpose of meriting the forgiveness of sins or righteousness. They instituted them for the sake of good order and tranquility in the church" (*BC* 216:13).

Lutheranism rejects any identification of the gospel with a particular polity, liturgy, or ethics. Word and sacraments are linked to adiaphora— earthly human ways which honor and guard the incarnation of God in Jesus of Israel. The form and function of what constitutes ecclesiastical authority may vary; it is never the same for all times. For the gospel cannot be guaranteed by the church, but only served. That is why Lutheranism, at its best and brightest, reflects the mystery of Christ rather than the contentiousness of an institution.

Luther symbolized his religious stance in a coat of arms known as the "Luther rose." It originated as a seal on a signet ring given to Luther by Elector Johann Frederick of Saxony in 1530 when the Augsburg Confession was submitted to Emperor Charles V. In the center of the seal is a black cross placed in a heart. The black cross symbolizes Christ's work in the believer, hurting yet healing human nature from the disease of sin. The heart is in the center of a white rose, symbolizing the joy and peace resulting from faith in Christ alone. The white rose is placed in a sky-blue field, symbolizing the heavenly future promised by Christ. Around the sky-blue field is a golden ring, symbolizing the never-ending love of God; it is precious like gold.

Being Lutheran means to focus on the cross of Christ in the heart. "Heart" is the biblical word for what makes humans tick, who they really are, and what they rely on. "For where your treasure is, there your heart will be also" (Matt. 6:21). The cross of Christ exorcises human life from the illusion of total individualism, from the sin of playing God. That is why the liturgy of baptism declares, "You have been marked with the cross of Christ forever." It is a constant reminder that the time between birth and death reflects the interim, the meantime, between Christ's first and second advent. Lutherans call this reminder "preaching the law." It is the admonition to people in the world that

Luther's Coat of Arms

they must be exorcised from the illusion of playing God and face the reality of life in obedience to God.

There is a dire need in the world, and in many churches, to face the realities of life under the conditions of death, sin, and evil. The legacy of Lutheranism discloses the enduring challenge to exorcise people from their favorite illusions and to invite them into the church as the gathering of those who embody the ancient, apostolic sense of the church as the "body of Christ" (1 Cor. 12:27). Its members are like ambassadors in a foreign land (2 Cor. 5:20), and even fools for the sake of Christ (1 Cor. 4:10). Lutherans know better than most Christians how to be resident aliens in the world. This status gives them a peculiar freedom and a doxological sense of life in the face of the joyful future promised by the gospel.

Lutherans have been more eager to guard the gospel from abuse than to embody its freedom and joy. They have been like German shepherd dogs in the dog-eat-dog world of denominationalism: They have more often hunted the enemy of the flock than enjoyed being with the shepherd. To be with Christ in word and sacrament means to have a foretaste of the feast that is to come, when "Christ is all and in all" (Col. 3:11).

An Introduction to the
Lutheran Confessions

◇

The Book of Concord: The Confessions of the Evangelical Lutheran Church. Theodore G. Tappert, ed. and trans. Philadelphia: Fortress Press, 1959. German edition: *Die Bekenntnisschriften der evangelisch-lutherischen Kirche.* 3rd ed. rev. Göttingen: Vandenhoeck & Ruprecht, 1956. Cited as *BC*.

The Book of Concord contains a collection of documents known as the "Lutheran Confessions," which are proposals for the reform of the medieval Roman Catholic Church and accounts of what Lutherans hold to be normative for Christian faith and life. The first part of *The Book of Concord* consists of the three trinitarian creeds of the ancient church (Apostles', Nicene, and Athanasian), followed by Martin Luther's Small and Large Catechisms of 1529; the Augsburg Confession of 1530; the Apology of the Augsburg Confession of 1531; the Schmalkald Articles of 1537; the Treatise on the Power and Primacy of the Pope of 1537; and the Formula of Concord of 1577. An appendix (only in the German and Latin editions) offers a "Catalogue of Testimonies From Scripture and the Ancient Pure Fathers of the Church."

The Small and Large Catechisms of 1529

Luther's catechisms are based on catechetical sermons preached in Wittenberg between 1523 and 1528, usually in May, September, and December. In addition, visitations in Saxony were conducted in 1527 and

1528 to diagnose church life among Lutherans. Four visitors made up a team that examined religious affairs and economic conditions. After Luther himself made visits to the Saxon countryside, he was shocked at the sloth of the clergy and the spiritual poverty of the laity. ("Good God, what wretchedness I beheld!" *BC* 338:2). He quickly published the Small Catechism for children and the Large Catechism for adults (first called German Catechism). The catechisms have five parts rather than the traditional three (decalogue, creed, Lord's Prayer). Luther added baptism and the Lord's Supper since he viewed the laity as partners in ministry with the ordained and thus should know basic Christian teachings. The Small Catechism concludes with forms for daily prayers and with instructions regarding the proper attitude toward ecclesiastical and political authorities.

The Augsburg Confession of 1530

Emperor Charles V invited the Lutheran reform party to state its case before the assembly of German princes at Augsburg on June 25, 1530. Luther's young friend and colleague, Philipp Melanchthon was asked to draft a statement since he was known for his diplomatic skill and irenic style (Luther called him a "soft-stepper," from the German *Leisetreter*). After much consultation, Melanchthon composed a two-part "confession" in German and in Latin. The first part summarizes teachings Lutherans had introduced in their territories with the help of governments in favor of reforms. These twenty-one "articles of faith and doctrine" affirm the dogma of the trinity (Articles 1–3), then assert salvation through Christ alone, by grace alone, by faith alone (Article 4). The other articles show how this Christocentric view reinterprets teachings about ministry, the church, sacraments, ecclesiastical and political government, ethics, and the cult of the saints (Articles 5–21). The second part of the confession lists "articles about matters in dispute" and shows how Lutherans have dealt with abuses. These seven articles defend communion in both kinds (the cup was denied to the laity), the marriage of priests, and the reform of public worship (Articles 22–24); they accept private confession, reject fasting and monastic vows (Articles 25–27); and contend for episcopacy in a renewed way (Article 28). Seven princes and two mayors signed the confession, claiming that it is in greater harmony with the Christian tradition than is the Roman Catholic Church.

The Apology of the Augsburg Confession of 1531

When Emperor Charles V rejected the Augsburg Confession, with the help of theologians siding with Rome, Melanchthon composed a lengthy defense, called an "apology" (from the Greek *apologia*, meaning "a speech in defense"), responding to the Roman theologians' Confutation. He offered the lengthiest and most passionate defense of the fourth article on justification (sixty pages), arguing once again how ecumenical Lutherans are in contrast to the Roman hierarchy. Melanchthon was a lay theologian committed to dialogue for Christian unity. By 1540 he had rewritten the Augsburg Confession (known as the "altered Augsburg Confession"), hoping to unite other Protestants with Lutherans. But Lutherans only accepted the unaltered Confession of 1530.

The Schmalkald Articles of 1537

These articles are Luther's theological testament, written for the Lutheran reform movement at a time when he thought he was dying: he had been seriously ill, suffering from kidney and gall stones as well as from heart problems. When Pope Paul III issued orders for a council of bishops to meet in Mantua, Italy, German Lutheran territories wanted Luther to draft a statement of faith worth dying for. Luther produced the statement and had it reviewed by other theologians before submitting it to the Saxon government. Saxony and other territories had formed a military league at Schmalkald in 1531 to defend the Lutheran cause against an attack by pope and emperor.

Luther's statement was to be adopted by the Schmalkald League at its assembly in the Thuringian town (ca. fifty miles southwest of Erfurt) in February of 1537. But the sick Luther went home before he could present the statement, and Melanchthon lobbied against it because he found it too polemical to unite all the members of the League. As a result, the Schmalkald Articles (as they were later called) were signed only by about forty Lutheran pastors and church leaders. Melanchthon signed with the condition that Lutherans would accept the authority of the pope as a symbol of Christian unity (*BC* 316–317).

In the first part of the articles, Luther affirmed the dogma of the trinity. In the second part, he asserted the unconditional authority of Christ in all aspects of faith and life (Article 2, 1). Then Luther condemned the Roman version of the Mass, the invocation of saints, monasteries, and the papacy (Article 2, 2–4). In the third part, Luther summarized his teachings focusing on sin, law, repentance, and the way the gospel functions in Christian life, ranging form baptism to ordination and ecclesiastical structures. (Article 3, 1–15).

The Treatise on the Power and Primacy of the Pope of 1537

Melanchthon wrote this treatise for the assembly of the Schmalkald league which adopted it as an amplification of the Augsburg Confession's statement on the power of bishops (Article 28).

Melanchthon rejected the Roman claims that the papacy was instituted by God through Christ's choice of Peter as the archetype of the papacy. He uses testimony from the Bible and from history to refute these claims. If popes continue to make such claims, he reasoned, they must be viewed as manifestations of the antichrist. The church, therefore, does not need popes but faithful bishops who are accountable to the whole church.

The Formula of Concord of 1577

After Luther's death in 1546, German Lutherans quarreled about ways in which Luther's theology should be doctrinally formulated. The disciples of Melanchthon sought formulations that might reconcile Wittenberg and Rome. Conservative Lutherans, led by Matthias Flacius, rejected all such attempts. Some tried to mediate since 1568, led by the Swabian Jakob Andreä whose sermons on concord created a basis for further efforts to unite the feuding factions. Supported by politicians, a convocation of theologians in Torgau, Saxony, produced the "Torgau Book" which was recast in 1577 as the Formula of Concord.

The document begins with a summary, entitled "Epitome," and lists the issues in the intra-Lutheran debates. They are to be settled in light of Scripture whose "prophetic and apostolic writings of the Old and New Testaments are the only rule and norm according to which all doctrines and teachers alike must be appraised" (*BC* 464:1). Then twelve issues are listed together with recommendations how to settle them: original sin, free will, righteousness of faith, good works, law and gospel, the third use of the law (whether Christians need laws), the Lord's

Supper, the person of Christ, Christ's descent into hell, adiaphora, divine election, and factions which are not committed to the Augsburg Confession. The full text of the Formula is called "Solid Declaration" and is signed by the six theologians who drafted it; by 1580, 8,188 other church leaders had signed it. On June 25, 1580, the Formula became the final part of *The Book of Concord*, commemorating the fiftieth anniversary of the Augsburg Confession. The signators of *The Book of Concord* want to be certain "that no adulterated doctrine might in the future be hidden [under the word of God] and that a pure declaration of the truth might be transmitted to our posterity as well" (*BC* 7).

A Guide to
Further Reading

◇

No published history of global Lutheranism exists. A general survey of Lutheran churches is offered by the Lutheran World Federation in E. Theodore Bachmann, and Mercia B. Bachmann. *Lutheran Churches in the World: A Handbook* Minneapolis: Augsburg, 1989.

A. Three works contain helpful general information about Lutheranism:

Bergendoff, Conrad. *The Church of the Lutheran Reformation: A Historical Survey.* St. Louis: Concordia, 1967.

Bodensieck, Julius, ed. *The Encyclopedia of the Lutheran Church.* 3 vols. Philadelphia: Fortress, 1965.

Swihart, Altmann K. *Luther and the Lutheran Church 1483–1960.* New York: Philosophical Library, 1960.

A massive collection of studies is contained in Paul D. Petersen, ed.; *Luther and Lutheranism.* A Bibliography Selected From the ATLA Religion Database, rev. ed. American Theological Library Association 1985.

B. There are histories of Lutheranism in various countries. They are uneven, varied, and represent the views of churches or individuals.

AUSTRALIA
Hebart, Theodore. *The United Evangelical Lutheran Church in Australia: Its History, Activities and Characteristics, 1839–1938.* North Adelaide: Lutheran Book Depot, 1938.

BRAZIL

Bachmann, Theodore E. *Lutherans in Brazil: A Story of Emerging Ecumenism.* Minneapolis, Augsburg, 1970.

CANADA

Cronmiller, Carl R. *A History of the Lutheran Church in Canada.* Kitchener, Ont.: Evangelical Lutheran Synod of Canada, 1961.

CHINA

Jonson, Jonas. *Lutheran Missions in a Time of Revolution: The Chinese Experience 1944–1951.* Uppsala: Tvavaga Forlage, 1972.

ENGLAND

Pearce, Edward G. *The Story of the Lutheran Church in Britain Through Four Centuries of History.* London: Evangelical Lutheran Church of England, 1969.

GERMANY

Dickens, A. G. *The German Nation and Martin Luther.* New York: Harper & Row, 1974.
Drummond, Andrew L. *German Protestantism Since Luther.* London: Epworth, 1951.

GUYANA

Beatty, Paul B. *A History of the Lutheran Church in Guyana.* Georgetown: Daily Chronicle, 1970.

INDIA

Swarley, C. H., ed. *The Lutheran Enterprise in India.* Madras: Diocesan Press, 1952.

INDONESIA

Cooley, Frank L. *Indonesia: Church and Culture.* New York: Friendship Press, 1968. Minimal material on Lutheranism.

JAPAN

Huddle, Benjamin P. *History of the Lutheran Church in Japan.* New York: United Lutheran Church in America, 1958.

KOREA

Ji, Won Yong. *A History of Lutheranism in Korea: A Personal Account.* Concordia Seminary Series 1. Seoul: Concordia, 1988.

MALAYSIA

Vierow, Duain W. *A History of Lutheranism in Western Malaysia and Singapore*. New York: Board of World Missions, Lutheran Church in America, 1968.

PAPUA NEW GUINEA

Wagner, Herwig and Hermann Reiner, eds. *The Lutheran Church in Papua New Guinea: The First Hundred Years 1886–1986*. Adelaide: Lutheran Publishing House, 1987.

RUSSIA

Duin, Edgar C. *Lutheranism Under the Tsars and the Soviets*. 2 vols. Ann Arbor: Xerox and University Microfilms, 1975.

SCANDINAVIA

Hunter, Leslie S. *Scandinavian Churches: A Picture of the Development and Life of the Churches of Denmark, Finland, Iceland, Norway, and Sweden*. London: Faber & Faber, 1965.

UNITED STATES

Nelson, Clifford E., ed. *The Lutherans in North America* 2d ed., rev. Philadelphia: Fortress, 1980.

Chapter 1: The Luther Event

There is a massive Luther literature based on 110 oversized volumes of Luther's work in German and Latin collected in the *Weimar Edition* (1883–   ). The English edition of Luther's works is available as: Pelikan, Jaroslav and Lehmann, Helmut T., eds. *Luther's Works*. 55 vols. Philadelphia: Fortress and St. Louis: Concordia, 1955–1986. This edition has been condensed in Lull, Timothy F. ed. *Martin Luther's Basic Theological Writings*. Minneapolis: Fortress, 1989.

A helpful history of the Reformation may be found in Spitz, Lewis W., *The Protestant Reformation 1517–1559*. The Rise of Modern Europe. New York: Harper & Row, 1985. Excellent bibliography. An enlightening Roman Catholic history is Lortz, Joseph. *The Reformation in Germany*. Translated by Ronald Wals. 2 vols. New York: Herder & Herder, 1968.

Three historical portraits of Luther disclose the breadth and depth of research and interpretation:

Brecht, Martin. *Martin Luther.* Translated by James L. Schaaf. 3 vols. Minneapolis: Fortress, 1990–93.

Gritsch, Eric W. *Martin—God's Court Jester: Luther in Retrospect.* 2d ed. Ramsey, N.J.: Sigler Press, 1990. Helpful bibliography.

Oberman, Heiko A. *Luther: Man Between God and the Devil.* Translated by Eileen Walliser-Schwarzbar. New Haven: Yale University Press, 1989.

Chapter 2: The Aborted Reformation

On the spread of Lutheranism to Scandinavia:

Bergendorff, Conrad. *Olavus Petri and the Ecclesiastical Transformation of Sweden: A Study in the Swedish Reformation.* New York: Macmillan, 1928.

Dunkley, E. H. *The Reformation in Denmark.* London: SPCK, 1948.

On the Council of Trent and the Lutheran reaction to it:

Chemnitz, Martin. *Examination of the Council of Trent.* Translated by Fred Kramer. St. Louis: Concordia, 1971. A Lutheran reaction by an orthodox second generation Lutheran theologian.

Jedin, Hubert. A History of the Council of Trent. Translated by Dom E. Graf. 2 vols. London: Nelson & Sons, 1954. A Roman Catholic account.

McNally, Robert E. *The Council of Trent, the Spiritual Exercises, and Catholic Reform.* Facet Book, Philadelphia: Fortress, 1970. A good, brief introduction to Trent, Loyola, and Roman Catholic reaction to the Reformation.

On Lutheran confessional developments:

Kolb, Robert. *Confessing the Faith: Reformers Define the Church, 1530–1580.* St. Louis: Concordia, 1991.

On Lutheran Orthodoxy:

Preus, Robert D. *The Theology of Post-Reformation Lutheranism.* St. Louis: Concordia, 1978.

On Lutheran Pietism:

Arden, Gothard E. *Four Northern Lights: Men Who Shaped Scandinavian Churches.* Minneapolis: Augsburg, 1964. Sketches of Grundtvig, Hauge, Rosenius, and Ruotsalinen.

Erb, Peter C., ed. *Pietists: Selected Writings.* The Classics of Western Spirituality. New York: Paulist Press, 1983. Introduction to and readings from German Pietists.

Guericke, Heinrich E. *The Life of August Hermann Francke*. Translated by Samuel Jackson. London: Bohn, 1847.

Lewis, Arthur J. *Zinzendorf, The Ecumenical Pioneer: A Study in the Moravian Contribution to Christian Mission and Unity*. Philadelphia: Westminster, 1962.

Nodtvedt, Magnus. *Rebirth of Norway's Peasantry: Folk Leader Hans Nielsen Hauge*. Tacoma: Pacific Lutheran University Press, 1965.

Spener, Philip J. *Pia Desideria* (Pious Desires). Edited and translated by Theodore G. Tappert. Philadelphia: Fortress, 1964. The manifesto of Lutheran Pietism.

On Gustavus Adolphus:

Fletcher, Charles R. *Gustavus Adolphus and the Thirty Years' War*. New York: Capricorn, 1963.

On Enlightenment and Lutheranism:

Cassirer, Ernst. *The Philosophy of the Enlightenment*. Translated by Fritz C. A. Koelln and James P. Pettegrove. Boston: Beacon, 1951. A classic, detailed account.

Cragg, Gerald R. *The Church and the Age of Reason 1648–1789*. Grand Rapids: Eerdmans, 1960. Helpful sketches of the age (ch. 4) and Lutheran reactions (chs. 7, 14).

On Lutheran theology:

Heick, Otto N. *A History of Christian Thought*. 2 vols. Philadelphia: Fortress, 1965. Volume II has sections on Schleiermacher and the various theological schools in Germany and Scandinavia.

Mackintosh, Hugh R. *Types of Modern Theology*. New York: Scribner's Sons, 1937. Textbook accounts of Schleiermacher, Hegel, Ritschl, and Kierkegaard.

Redeker, Martin. *Schleiermacher: Life and Thought*. Translated by John Wallhauser. Philadelphia: Fortress, 1973.

Sykes, Stephen. *Friedrich Schleiermacher*. Richmond: John Knox, 1971. An introduction to Schleiermacher.

Chapter 3: Old World Network

On the industrial revolution and economics:

Marx, Karl. *Capital, Communist Manifesto and Other Writings*. Edited by Max Eastmann. New York: Modern Library, 1932.

Smith, Adam. *An Inquiry into the Nature and Causes of the Wealth of Nations.* Chicago: Encyclopedia Britannica, 1955. The classic argument for capitalism.

On Nietzsche:

Hollingdale, R. J. *Nietzsche: The Man and His Philosophy.* Baton Rouge: Louisiana State University Press, 1965.

Jaspers, Karl. *Nietzsche and Christianity.* Translated by E. B. Ashton. Chicago: Regnery, 1961. An evaluation by an agnostic mind.

Riessen, H. van. *Nietzsche.* Translated by D. Jellema. Grand Rapids: Baker House, 1960. A brief introduction to Nietzsche.

On Darwin:

Ruse, Michael. *The Darwinian Revolution: Science Red in Tooth and Claw.* Chicago: University of Chicago Press, 1979. Good bibliography.

On the Salzburgers:

Strobel, Philip D. *The Salzburgers and Their Descendants.* Athens: University of Georgia Press, 1953.

On Lutheran reactions to new trends:

Vidler, Alec R. *The Church in an Age of Revolution: 1789 to the Present Day.* Grand Rapids: Eerdmans, 1961. Chs. 2, 8–9, 18.

On Grundtvig.

Knudsen, Johannes. *Danish Rebel: A Study of N. F. Grundtvig.* Philadelphia: Muhlenberg, 1955.

On Kierkegaard:

Fear and Trembling: A good way to begin reading Kierkegaard.

Allen, Edgar C. *Kierkegaard: His Life and Thought.* London: Nott, 1935. Standard biography.

Diem, Hermann. *Kierkegaard: An Introduction.* Translated by David Green. Richmond: John Knox, 1966.

On "Inner Mission":

Bradfield, Margaret. *The Good Samaritan: The Life and Work of Friedrich von Bodelschwingh.* London: Marshall, 1964.

Christianson, Gerald. "J. H. Wichern and the Rise of the Lutheran Social Institution." *Lutheran Quarterly* 19 (1967): 357–70.

Ohl, Jeremiah F. *The Inner Mission: A Handbook for Christian Workers.* Philadelphia: General Council, 1911. Helpful historical information.

Chapter 4: New World Immigrants

The best source is the collective work of scholars edited by Nelson, E. Clifford and Theodore G. Tappert, et al. *Lutherans in North America.* Philadelphia: Fortress, 1975. Index and bibliography are very helpful.

On the influence of Löhe:

Heintzen, Eric H. *Love Leaves Home: Wilhelm Löhe and the Missouri Synod.* St. Louis: Concordia, 1973.

Löhe, Wilhelm. *Three Books on the Church.* Translated and edited by James L. Schaaf. Philadelphia: Fortress, 1969.

Schober, Theodor. *Treasure Houses of the Church: The Formation of the Diaconate Through the Lutherans Wilhelm Löhe, Hermann Bezzel, and Hans Lauerer.* Translated by Bertha Moeller and edited by Frederick S. Weiser. Typescript, Library, Gettysburg Lutheran Seminary.

Weiser, Fredrick S. *Love's Response. A Story of Lutheran Deaconesses in America.* Philadelphia: Board of Publication, United Lutheran Church in America, 1962.

On Muhlenberg:

Muhlenberg, Henry. *The Journals of Henry Melchior Muhlenberg.* Translated by Theodore G. Tappert and John W. Doberstein. Philadelphia: Evangelical Lutheran Ministerium of Pennsylvania and Adjacent States, 1942–1958. Reprint by the Lutheran Historical Society of Eastern Pennsylvania, Evansville, IL: Whippoorvill Publications, 1982. Fascinating.

Riforgiato, Leonard. K. *Missionary of Moderation: Henry Melchior Muhlenberg and the Lutheran Church in English America.* Lewisburg: Bucknell University Press, 1980.

On Schmucker:

Schmucker, Samuel. *Fraternal Appeal to the American Churches, With a Plea for Catholic Union on Apostolic Principles.* Edited by Frederick K. Wentz, Philadelphia: Fortress, 1965. A seminal document of American Lutheranism.

Wentz, Abdel R. *Pioneer in Christian Unity: Samuel Simon Schmucker.* Philadelphia: Fortress, 1967. Bibliography and list of Schmucker's writings.

On Walther:

Spitz, Lewis W. *The Life of Dr. C. F. W. Walther.* St. Louis: Concordia, 1961.

Walther, C. F. W. *Selected Letters.* Edited by Carl S. Meyer. St. Louis: Concordia, 1973.
On Polity:
Fortenbaugh, Robert. *The Development of the Synodical Polity of the Lutheran Church in America, to 1829.* Philadelphia: Author's publication, 1926.

Chapter 5: Missionary Connections

On Tranquebar, India:
Lehmann, Arno. *Tranquebar: The Story of the Tranquebar Mission and the Beginnings of Protestant Christianity in India.* Translated by M. J. Lutz. Madras: Christian Literature Society, 1956.
Zorn, H. M. *Bartholomaeus Ziegenbalg.* St. Louis: Concordia, 1933.
On the Batak Church:
Anderson, Gerald H., ed. *Asian Voices in Christian Theology.* New York: Orbis, 1976. Appendix has text of Batak Confession.
Burgess, Andrew S., ed. *Lutheran Churches in the Third World.* Minneapolis: Augsburg, 1970. Essays on Japan, China, Taiwan, Hong Kong, Korea, Southeast Asia, India, Middle East, Africa, Latin America.
On South Africa:
Enquist, Roy J. *Namibia: Land of Tears, Land of Promise.* Selinsgrove: Susquehanna University Press, 1990. Shows the influence of Lutheranism. Written just before Namibia became independent.

Chapter 6: World Lutheranism

Nelson, Clifford E. *The Rise of World Lutheranism: An American Perspective.* Philadelphia: Fortress, 1982. The best resource on world Lutheranism.
On Söderblom:
Curtis, Charles J. *Söderblom: Ecumenical Pioneer.* Minneapolis: Augsburg, 1971.
Sundkler, Bengt G. *Nathan Söderblom: His Life and Work.* Lund: Gleerup, 1968.
On Lutherans and Nazism:
Conway, John S. *The Nazi Persecution of the Church 1933–45.* New York: Basic Books, 1968.

Helmreich, Ernst Ch. *The German Church Under Hitler: Background, Struggle, Epilogue.* Detroit: Wayne State University Press, 1979.

Hoeye, Bjarne and Ager, Trygve M. *The Fight of the Norwegian Church Against Nazism.* New York: Macmillan, 1943.

Hoeye, Bjarne and Ager, Trygve and Locke, Hubert G., ed. *The German Church Struggle and the Holocaust.* Detroit: Wayne State University Press, 1974. Sixteen essays by Christians and Jews.

Littell, Franklin H. *The German Phoenix.* New York: Doubleday, 1960. Appendix: Texts of the Platform of German Christians (1932), the Barmen Declaration (1934), and the Stuttgart Declaration (1945).

Scholder, Klaus. *The Church and the Third Reich.* Translated by John Bowden. 2 vols. Philadelphia: Fortress, 1988. Covers the period from 1918–34. Author died before completing the third volume.

On Niemöller:

Bentley, James. *Martin Niemoeller, 1892–1984.* Oxford: Oxford University Press, 1989.

Niemöller, Martin. *From U-Boat to Pulpit.* Translated by Hastig Smith. New York: Willett, Clark & Co., 1927. Niemöller's account. See appendix: "From Pulpit to Prison."

On Bonhoeffer:

Bethge, Eberhard. *Dietrich Bonhoeffer: Man of Vision, Man of Courage.* Edited by Eric Mosbacher et al. Edwin H. Robertson. New York: Harper & Row, 1970.

Bonhoeffer, Dietrich. *The Cost of Discipleship.* Translated by Reginald H. Fuller and revised by Irmgard Booth. New York: Macmillan, 1963. Bonhoeffer's most popular work.

————, *Costly Grace: An Illustrated Introduction to Dietrich Bonhoeffer.* Translated by Rosaleen Ockenden. New York: Harper & Row, 1979.

Kelly, Geffrey B. and Nelson, Burton F.; eds. *A Testament to Freedom: The Essential Writings of Dietrich Bonhoeffer.* San Francisco: Harper, 1990.

Rasmussen, Larry. *Dietrich Bonhoeffer: His Significance for North America.* Chapter 1 by Renate Bethge, translated by Geffrey B. Kelly. Philadelphia: Fortress, 1990.

On Lutheran World Federation:

"Helsinki 1963." *Lutheran World* 11 (1964): 1–36. The debate on "justification" at the Fourth Assembly of LWF: " 'Justification Today,'

Document 75—Assembly and Final Versions." *Lutheran World* 12, 1, Supplement (1965): 1–11.

The Seventh Assembly in Budapest 1984: *LWF Report* 19/20 (1985).

The work of LWF is published in *Lutheran World* and its successor *LWF Report*.

Thekaekava, Marie M. *Fireflies in the Night: Glimpses of the Lutheran World Service, 1975–1982.* Calcutta: Christ's Disciples' Media, 1983.

Vajta, Vilmos. *From Generation to Generation: The LWF 1947–1982.* Geneva: Kreuzverlag, 1983.

Chapter 7: Proper God-talk

On Lutheran Theology in general:

Braaten, Carl E. *Principles of Lutheran Theology.* Philadelphia: Fortress, 1983. Brief, hard-hitting essays.

Braaten, Carl E. and Jenson, Robert W. *Christian Dogmatics.* 2 vols. Philadelphia: Fortress, 1984. An extensive "systematic theology" produced by a team of six Lutheran theologians in the United States. Helpful bibliography and indexes.

Elert, Werner. *The Structure of Lutheranism.* Vol. 1, *The Theology and Philosophy of Life of Lutheranism, Especially in the Sixteenth and Seventeenth Centuries.* Translated by Walter A. Hansen. St. Louis: Concordia, 1962. An older German, conservative work. The untranslated second volume sketches the history of Lutheranism.

Gritsch, Eric W. and Jenson, Robert W. *Lutheranism: The Theological Movement and Its Confessional Writings.* Philadelphia: Fortress, 1976. A popular exposition of the theology of the Lutheran Confessions and their ecumenical dimensions.

On God-talk:

Braaten, Carl E. *Justification: The Article by Which the Church Stands and Falls.* Minneapolis: Fortress, 1990.

Dantine, Wilhelm, *The Justification of the Ungodly.* Translated by Eric W. Gritsch & Ruth C. Gritsch. St. Louis: Concordia, 1968.

Elert, Werner. *Law and Gospel.* Translated by Edward H. Schroeder. Philadelphia: Fortress, 1967.

Forde, Gerhard O. *Justification by Faith—A Matter of Death and Life.* Philadelphia: Fortress, 1982.

Chapter 8: Life in the Meantime

Brand, Eugene L. *Baptism: A Pastoral Perspective.* Minneapolis: Augsburg, 1975.

Duchrow, Ulrich. *Two Kingdoms: The Use and Misuse of a Lutheran Theological Concept.* Geneva: Lutheran World Federation, 1977.

Hauerwas, Stanley and Willimon, William. *Resident Aliens.* Nashville: Abingdon, 1989.

Hertz, Karl H., ed. *Two Kingdoms and One World: A Sourcebook in Christian Social Ethics.* Minneapolis: Augsburg, 1976.

Lazareth, William. H. *Luther on the Christian Home: An Application of the Social Ethics of the Reformation.* Philadelphia: Muhlenberg, 1960.

Chapter 9: Formation for Mission

On Worship:

Gritsch, Eric W., ed. "Luther: Worship and Liturgical Renewal." In *Encounters with Luther.* 4 vols., 2:5–27. Gettysburg: Institute for Luther Studies, 1982.

Luther, Martin. *Liturgy and Hymns.* Vol. 53 of American Edition.

Vajta, Vilmos. *Luther on Worship: An Interpretation.* Translated by U.S. Leupold. Philadelphia: Muhlenberg, 1958.

On Education:

Gritsch, Eric W., ed. "Luther and Parish Education." In *Encounters with Luther.* 4 vols. 2:236–82. Gettysburg: Institute for Luther Studies, 1982.

Jenson, Robert W. *A Large Catechism.* Mt. Vernon, NY: American Lutheran Publicity Bureau, 1990. An interpretation of Luther's Large Catechism.

Lutheran Education: A journal dealing with various issues and answers.

Repp, Arthur C. *Luther's Catechism Comes to America: Theological Effects on the Issues of the Small Catechism Prepared in or for America Prior to 1850.* ATLA monograph Series 18. Metuchen, NJ: Scarecrow Press, 1982. Shows how un-Lutheran catechetics dominated Lutheran education in congregations.

On ethics:

Althaus, Paul. *The Ethics of Martin Luther.* Translated by Robert C. Schultz. Philadelphia: Fortress, 1972. Companion volume to *The The-*

ology of Martin Luther. Translated by Robert C. Schultz. Philadelphia: Fortress, 1966.

Bonhoeffer, Dietrich. *Ethics.* Edited by Eberhard Bethge and translated by Horton Smith. New York: Macmillan, 1955. The work of the German martyr from the 1940s.

Gritsch, Eric W., ed. "Luther and the Moral Question." In *Encounters with Luther.* 4 vol. 1:217–70. Gettysburg: Institute for Luther Studies, 1980.

Chapter 10: The Gift of Unity

Materials on Christian unity focus on dialogue between churches, especially since the 1960s. The most consistent and exemplary one is the Lutheran-Roman Catholic Dialogue in North America which has had nine rounds. Its latest publication is Burgess, Joseph A., et al eds. *The Word of God: Scripture and Tradition.* Minneapolis: Augsburg, 1993. A helpful summary of the work of Lutheran dialoguers is Burgess, Joseph A., *In Search of Christian Unity: Basic Consensus/Basic Difference.* Minneapolis: Fortress, 1991.

On Lutheranism and unity:

Empie, Paul C. *Lutherans and Catholics in Dialogue: Personal Notes for a Study.* Edited by Raymond Tiemeyer. Philadelphia: Fortress, 1981. Helpful reflections on the Lutheran pioneer of the Lutheran-Catholic dialogue.

Gritsch, Eric W., ed. "Luther, the Church and Christian Unity" and "Luther and the Christian Tradition." In *Encounters with Luther.* 4 vols. 3:114–172; 177–221. Gettysburg: Institute for Luther Studies, 1986.

Rusch, William G. *Ecumenism—A Movement Toward Church Unity.* Philadelphia: Fortress, 1985.

Scherer, James. *Mission and Unity in Lutheranism.* Philadelphia: Fortress, 1969.

BX8018 .G75 1994   CU-Main

Gritsch, Eric W./Fortress introduction to Lutheran

3 9371 00012 2622

◇——— A C K N ▌▌▌▌▌▌▌▌▌▌▌▌▌▌ E N T S ———◇

———————————◇———————————

The photo of Martin Niemöller on page 89 is reprinted from *Pastor Niemöller* by Dietmar Schmidt (Garden City, N.Y.: Doubleday and Co., 1959).

The photo on page 84 is reprinted by permission of the Archives of Cooperative Lutheranism, 8765 W. Higgins Rd., Chicago, IL 60631-4198.

The photo on page 92 is reprinted by permission of the Lutheran World Federation Archives.

The photo on page 88 is reprinted by permission of the Keystone Agency, Hamburg, Germany.

The photo of Dietrich Bonhoeffer on page 89, copyright © Chr. Kaiser/ Gütersloher Verlagshaus, Gütersloh, is reprinted by permission.